Free to Be Me

The Joy of Finding Your True Self

NEVA COYLE

... The most courageous act is to still think for yourself ...

KINGSWAY PUBLICATIONS
EASTBOURNE

ISBN 0 85476 875 0

Published by
KINGSWAY PUBLICATIONS
Lottbridge Drove, Eastbourne, BN23 6NT, England.
E-mail: books@kingsway.co.uk

Designed and produced for the publishers by
Bookprint Creative Services, P.O. Box 827, BN21 3YJ, England.
Printed in Great Britain.

Reproduced from the original text by arrangement with
Servant Publications.

Contents

Introduction / 5

1. Where Did the Real Me Go? / 11

2. Leaving the Real Me Behind / 27

3. How Do I Get the Real Me Back? / 38

4. In the Company of One / 52

5. Making Time for the Real Me / 65

6. You Are a "Work of Heart" / 76

7. Changing the Real Me / 86

8. Honoring the Real Me / 101

9. Nurturing the Real Me / 110

10. Honoring Your Real Needs / 119

11. Honoring Your Body / 132

12. Honoring God From the Heart of the Real Me / 141

Notes / 158

Introduction

"Hey, Mom! Where's my gym shirt?"

It's your quiet time ... and just when a certain phrase or passage of Scripture seems as if it's God's personal promise, someone needs something. *I'll get them off to school, and I'll come back for a few more minutes before I leave for work.* The promise is made as much to yourself as it is to the Lord. But then life *really* hits.

"Where's my homework?"

"I need a permission slip."

"Janie's mom can't drive after school and we need a ride to dance class."

"Honey, they can take the car this morning at nine. How's that work with your day?"

"Don't forget to take the dog to the vet."

You manage to get them out the door and head for the shower before stuffing the washing machine full of dirty towels.

You still have forty-five minutes before your first appointment. Setting the dial on the washing machine, you head for your promised devotional rendezvous.

As you stand with the blow dryer in one hand and your Bible in the other, the phone rings.

"I forgot my lunch money."

Life happens to you. If it's not the kids and hubby, a hundred other distractions fill your crowded calendar. Soon you're on "over" load—overfunctioning and overresponsible—and just getting through the day leaves you exhausted.

Many of us suffer from the "terrible too's." We are: *too busy, too available, too perfect, too in demand, too dependable, too out-of-touch with our selves and our real needs.*

Unfortunately, we soon become emotionally drained and spiritually undernourished. We become too sensitive to criticism, and too resistant to suggestions that we slow down or simplify our lives. And all the time we wonder: Shouldn't there be *some* room for our own needs, and for personal growth? How do we get so bound up in our adrenaline-driven lives?

Not long ago, the pace of life caught up with me. I'd given all I could give. I found myself looking in the mirror and wondering, *Who are you anyway?* I had become my responsibilities—which included a household to run, writing deadlines, church activities, a speaking schedule, radio interviews, friendships to maintain, and family communications. Take a day off? Indulgent. Curl up with a good book for a whole day? Impossible.

Am I so different from other busy women? I don't think so. We are legion. It's no wonder thousands of us have lost the sense of being our real selves, when everything in our world pressures us to base our personal identity and worth on what we *do*—especially what we do for others—rather than on who we *are*. The *real me* is covered up—and replaced—by the *doing me*.

If you sense that you have lost your real self, I suggest that what you're feeling is really a prompting from our heavenly Father. A nudge that something within you needs to change.

Consider it: *Who are you?*

While you're thinking, I want to remind you of some truths you may have forgotten. You see, there is no one else quite like you. You are a unique collection of emotions, opinions, talents, creativity, and passions. You have come through both pain-filled and happy experiences. Very likely, you've gathered more than a little wisdom by now. You hold tightly to certain spiritual beliefs.

Yet, what do you answer when someone asks, "Who are you?" "I'm Suzie's mother." "I'm Jack's wife." Or you say, "I'm a schoolteacher," or "I'm a legal secretary." Do you respond by listing the positions you hold, the responsibilities you carry, or the roles you fill? Have you come to think in terms of *what you do* and *who you serve* rather than *who you are* as a basis for your identity and even your worth?

Too many of us have become attached to what we think we ought to *do*, forgetting what we've been designed by God to *be*. We push through our busy, demanding lives. We're satisfied with being productive. But we live as missing persons.

It's no wonder that in spite of family, friends, work, and church activities we sometimes feel alone and out of place.

What's more, it's my belief that one of the reasons we feel so alone is that we haven't made it our priority to discover who we really are. We operate so easily out of *roles*, we rarely consider our *real selves*.

How do we reconcile this problem—being so busy, yet feeling so far from ourselves? And what's the root of our dilemma?

In this book, I want to help you recognize forces in your life that keep you from being who you are. I want to help you discover the person God has made you to be, and help you find greater spiritual health. In these pages, I'd like to introduce you to a surprising person—*you*. Furthermore, I'll introduce you to a wonderful way to become better acquainted with yourself and your personal gifts.

This trip into your heart will not be taken unassisted. God's Word will be your guide, and the Holy Spirit your companion. On occasion, you may discover a point that reveals the need to visit with a mentor or trusted friend. Some of you may even discover the need for professional guidance or counseling.

God has some wonderful things to show you about the investment of His creativity within you, and what He had in mind as He formed you in your mother's womb (see Ps 139). The experience that lies just ahead on these pages can also lead you into a depth of personal relationship with Christ that you may never have experienced before.

Your "supplies" for this journey will be very basic. In addition to this book, you will need a Bible. I also recommend that you keep a personal journal to record your thoughts and prayers. Plan a half hour or more each day for personal exploration, and choose a place where you can be alone.

My desire is that, by the time you reach the end of this book, you'll be a much better personal friend to yourself than ever before. Don't be surprised if you sense a new contentment springing up within. There's a good chance that your husband or other family members will comment that you are much more fun and easier to get along with. Your friends might even mention how much more at peace you seem. The Lord will seem closer and your relationship with Him will feel more secure than ever. As a result of this experience you may even discover more courage and strength surging within as you face your challenging life and its difficult situations.

Have you been asking, "What ever happened to the real me?" The answer can be found by embracing the quiet and soul-enriching dynamic of solitude … and meeting your true self in the presence of God. It has been my delightful experience that "alone time" in God's presence is one of the most effective strategies we can use to regain our unique individuality.

And so as we begin, I pray that you will let the Holy Spirit use this book to gently guide you to find the person who is most often missing in your life—*the real you*.

ONE

Where Did the Real Me Go?

My photograph, at nine months of age, shows a smiling, happy baby with a bubbly personality. My mother tells me that even at that age I was outgoing, friendly, and well dispositioned.

My picture at five is quite different. A pensive, fearful child stares up at you from the shiny paper. What happened to this little person in between those two photo sessions is a case history in the way early childhood experiences can drive the real you into hiding.

But wait. I'm not a child anymore. And I can hear the protests that have become loud today. *So you had a lousy childhood. You're an adult. Let the past stay in the past. Get over it.* Those who think this way overlook the fact that "getting over it" is not a one-time event. It's a process: a journey that requires us, first, to face the influences—from family, friends,

church, culture—that have shaped us ... and maybe even sabotaged the *real person* God created us to be. This process I
know well, because as an adult I discovered that parts of my
true personhood had been pushed aside, feeding a dull grief
inside, a nagging sense that life was missing something.

More importantly, I found that the missing pieces of myself
were still there, waiting to be reclaimed! I found that, with
God's help, I could become the real me, no matter my age
(let's just say midlife) and no matter what changes had to be
made in my life (many, many).

My goal is to help you do the same.

The Miracle of Me—The Real Me in the Making

For you created my inmost being; you knit me together in
my mother's womb. I praise you because I am fearfully and
wonderfully made; your works are wonderful, I know that
full well. My frame was not hidden from you when I was
made in the secret place. When I was woven together in the
depths of the earth, your eyes saw my unformed body. All
the days ordained for me were written in your book before
one of them came to be.

PSALM 139:13-16

For most of her life, Jacque could not relate to the idea of
being "fearfully and wonderfully made" by God. She had the
strange, secret sensation that she wasn't quite who she was
supposed to be. Even as an adult, she sometimes felt "lost."

She was aware that she had long ignored her authentic self in order to fit into her family's expectations. But, she asked herself, isn't that how it has to be?

Where did Jacque learn that she had to erase herself and become what other people wanted her to be?

"They wanted a boy," she told me over coffee. Her mother had been warned not to have any more children, but she became pregnant, hoping to produce a longed-for son for Jacque's father. The little girl was a disappointment. And there could be absolutely no more children. "She pushed me to be boyish. I was taught to be tougher, rougher, and less feminine than my sisters. Somehow, I always felt *I* was supposed to make up for the son Mom felt she owed my dad."

I studied the thick blonde hair, the near-perfect face, the mysterious deep brown eyes. The beautiful woman across the table from me certainly didn't appear to be someone whose femininity had been discouraged.

"It was a terrible burden," Jacque continued. "I tried to be my dad's buddy. But I ended up seething with resentment over the way he treated my sisters, like his precious darlings. He treated me rougher, almost too rough. I was jealous."

Yet the person I knew was not resentful, bitter, or full of grief. How did Jacque find a way out of the role she'd had to play? How did this confident, happy woman emerge?

What unfolded was a story of forgiveness and prayer … and of a woman who learned to let God reveal her true self. "Little by little, I embraced what my parents had tried to deny me—my God-given right to be myself. They didn't plan on another daughter, but God designed me to be a woman. It has taken

me a long time, but I intend to enjoy the miracle of who I am
... to the limit!"

A Natural-Born Miracle

Just like Jacque, you are a miracle! Whether you were conceived
through the careful and prayerful planning of loving and godly
parents, or by two uncaring or unprepared adults, you are a miracle. God attended your very conception, hovered over your
early prenatal development, and watched over your birth.

Even as your blood, tissues, and bones were forming inside
your mother's womb, God's blueprinted instructions that
determined your height, weight, and coloring were being followed to a T. Everything about you was predetermined: Who
you would resemble. How you would move your hands when
gesturing while you talk. Your talents and disposition. Even
how you would carry your body and the length of your gait. It
was all coded within the genes, imprinted within your DNA,
and divinely fused at your conception. You were born to be the
real you. An absolute miracle.

But ... it's easy to read those words and apply them to someone else. All I had to do was look at my beautiful children to
know instantly that the poetic wisdom of Psalm 139 surely
applied to them. Yet for much of my past I believed these
words—some of the most beautiful in all the Bible—could not
possibly apply to me. I actually lived most of my early life feeling more like a piece of trash. A white elephant foisted on my
family. An embarrassment.

Like Jacque, I was well into my adult years, and seeking to deepen my relationship with Jesus Christ, before I began to realize how unique, loved, and wanted I actually was. After years of believing my worth was tied to other people's standards, demands, wishes, and whims, I came to understand *the miracle God made me to be at birth, and what a miracle my life continues to be.* Can you say the same?

Do you realize that your birth had more to do with God's plan than with your parents' ideas? What's happened to His designs and plans for a unique person? *What ever happened to the real you?*

Many women I know were simply overlooked and ignored. While the pretty, talented, or outgoing girls grabbed all the attention, they were brushed aside. "I loved music and painting," says Carrie, "but no one ever took an interest in me, or encouraged me." Other women grew up in overly strict or religiously legalistic homes. They were denied the right to their own opinions, their own chance to live and to grow by learning and making mistakes. *There could be no mistakes. It was selfish to think of your own needs.* Still others were simply told from the outset, "You *will* become ... such and such." Their life was mapped, their destiny set by someone else.

There are countless ways we get the message that it's OK to be here but it isn't OK to be who we really are.

Many Christian women bear scars from growing up in an environment where religious ideals are used in a confining or harmful way. Leslie feels both physically inept and cheated. She wanted to pursue sports, but was denied because sports were considered "trivial" and "worldly." Carole was forbidden to take part in after-school activities and clubs because her parents and church held the conviction that "Christian" kids should not mix too much with "worldly" kids. Marie was taught to subordinate all her thoughts, opinions, and desires to those of her husband: Whatever he thought, she was to think; whatever he liked, she was to like.

Such massive denials of self leave women searching for a true self. Worse, they leave scars where the person God created should be. They leave hollow women who have forced themselves into "acceptable roles"—women who live with empty holes inside where fulfilled dreams should be.

It's time that all this denial of self came to an end.

A Journey Together

This book is written with love and understanding for you, the reader. I have prayerfully set these words to paper, knowing I must be willing to be open about my own rediscovery and the reclaiming of my authenticity; knowing I must be honest about the costs of doing so. I hope to help you make the same choices and find the same staggering joy and reality that I have found.

This will be an intensely and personally revealing book for both of us. I count the revelation of my own inward search and discovery, as personal and private as it is, a true joy if it helps you once and for all come to know and be the authentic person you were created to be.

How do we find our true self?

To do that, we begin at the beginning. The true beginning of all that is. Take a moment to meditate on the profound truths we read in Psalm 139:15:

My frame was not hidden from you when I was made in the secret place.

Do you realize what the psalmist is saying? The "secret place" was not only your mother's womb, it was also in the depths of God's heart. It was in the depths of His being that the Father mused over you, paid careful attention to your design and development. Tiny arm-buds sprouted into limbs, legs lengthened, and every encoded detail came together to make you a physical and emotional being. God labored over you, putting together the woman He wanted you to be.

Where Was God When ...

Sometimes we reject ourselves because others have rejected us. We live with a deep sense of wariness, afraid to trust our own instincts because no place, no one, seems safe.

We read passages like Isaiah 43:1-5 with a question mark in our heads:

But now, this is what the Lord says—he who created you, O Jacob, he who formed you, O Israel: "Fear not, for I have redeemed you; I have summoned you by name; you are mine. When you pass through the waters, I will be with you; and when you pass through the rivers, they will not sweep over you. When you walk through the fire, you will not be burned; the flames will not set you ablaze. For I am the Lord, your God, the Holy One of Israel, your Savior ... Since you are precious and honored in my sight, and because I love you, I will give [the wicked] ... in exchange for your life. Do not be afraid, for I am with you."

Reading these strong promises of protection, I myself have been forced to wonder: Where was God during much of my childhood? Where was He during the events that left me feeling anything but wanted and protected, unsure of my own instincts, unsure of myself?

I know about the torment of being utterly rejected, the object of hatred and ridicule. When I was three, barely ready for normal and healthy separation from my mother, the cruelty began. Not at the hands of an adult, but at the hands of my older sisters. They talked me into putting my finger in a light-bulb socket. They stuck theirs in first, and nothing happened. "Come on, don't be afraid."

I'll never forget the agonizing jolt that whirred through my entire body.

My mother was furious, and I'm sure my sisters were spanked. But I'd been singled out. Was it because I was littler? More vulnerable? Why *do* you choose to hate a three-year-old?

Sometime later, they presented me with two bare electrical wires. I was not as eager to believe them, but they were so convincing. "Do you think we want to get in trouble again?" I chose to trust my older sisters. This time the electrical surge threw me to the bare cement floor. Afterward, they led me out back, just out of view of the house. There I was shown a fresh mound of dirt surrounded with carefully placed rocks and a small cross made from sticks.

"If you tell on us," my older sister said, "we'll kill you. We've already killed one little girl and we buried her right here."

"Yeah," the other sister said, "we shocked her to death."

I did not tell. At that moment, I abandoned myself. I had no idea what I was doing, but, dramatic as it sounds, I gave myself into the hands of two people who seemed to have the power of life and death over me.

Over the next few months, the psychological abuse began. "You're not really part of the family. Mom and Dad took you in because you were an orphan. They really don't want you, and if they find some place that will take you they'll send you away." So they gained another power over me. I did whatever they wanted, thinking I needed to be "good" in order to earn the right to stay in "their" house. If I didn't do what they said there would be no birthday present, no Christmas present. I was shut in the house. Shut out of the house. They hid until I was nearly hysterical at the thought I had been abandoned … then told me one day I'd be left all alone anyway, so I'd better get used to it.

I now understand how my hardworking parents could remain oblivious to these things. They scratched out an existence for our family in the California desert. Mom and Dad raised chickens, and Dad took paying jobs whenever possible. Dad's mother lay for days on end in a small cabinlike structure next to our house, suffering with tuberculosis, and the burden of her constant care lay heavily on my mother. By necessity, they left me in the care of the older two girls. It's what families did to manage. Mom—and the care, protection, nurturing, and affirmation I needed to grow—was working or taking care of Grandma, and always just beyond my reach.

I tell you this because it's my earliest remembrance. From this point on, I believed it was not all right to be me. It was not OK to need or want anything. I lived tentatively. Scared. Wanting only to fit in and please. While this was the first time I set my real me aside, it certainly was not the last.

As I have said, many of us formed this pattern in childhood, learning to push our true selves aside. My friend Sherrie says:

"I was the last in a line of five kids. One girl and four older brothers. I was teased and tormented continually, and no one stood up for me. My brothers broke my toys and loved to make me cry. They made fun of my dolls and called me a sissy. 'Oh, look,' they'd say, 'the little mommy.' It wasn't the words, it was the tone they used. As if being a little girl and doing all the little girl things was wrong or shameful."

So, as an adult Christian woman, I stare long and hard at the promises God made through Isaiah: "I will be with you...." Did He love *me* enough not to abandon me, when I felt so worthless, so unacceptable? Certainly Sherrie and I aren't the only women who have asked this question.

Where We Begin

It's at this point—where I am most likely to doubt God's love and His presence—that I must begin the journey to recover my true self with a step of faith. And so must you. The truth of

God's Word isn't validated by our experiences. believe it or not, whether we *feel* it to be true, God's absolute truth. Even though I hadn't yet heard these gr promises, God was at work to see me through. Before I was old enough to start school, He was there to make sure I wasn't overwhelmed and destroyed by the cruelty of others. He was in the words and in the loving eyes of my mom's mother, who, in her Sunday school class, taught me to give my heart to Jesus. I did, gladly, and all the awful feelings of worthlessness that came with the abuse were offset by the knowledge that *God loved me*. Even if I didn't belong to this family, I could, I would, belong forever to God.

Thus I can say that, even in my own personal fire and flood, God was with me.

Just as He has always been with you.

The God of Your Past Is Still Present

When was the first time you set aside your real self?

Monica always felt it was her job to make everyone else happy—never mind what *she* wanted. For Alyce, the self-denial began when her child's severe illness seemed to dictate that she grab the highest-paying job, with the best benefits, and forget her own dreams. For Jamie, it was when she was pushed by her husband and church into giving up a career because it was expected that she stay home and care for her two small step-sons. For Kathy, it was when she was browbeaten into silence when she wanted to be trained as an investment broker and she

-secretary. For Wendy, it started
...n of a simple, settled, country life
...reer path, which drags them to a new
neighborhood, every other year.

...ome circumstance, seem to deny you the
...ant, to question?

God ... .bandoned us, though we have abandoned
ourselves. His promise to bring us through all that is set against
us is true. Maybe you were given a poor start as a child, with
no opportunities, but the promise of God's help applies today.
Maybe someone you loved and trusted took part of your self
away by neglect or abuse, but God can love you back to wholeness and fulfillment.

As you reconsider events and choices that have, so far, kept
you from becoming your true self, be ready to take a new
"stand." You see, no one had God's permission to rob you of
your dreams, your goals, your self. Today you can grow
stronger in spirit by accepting this assurance—that God wants
to restore your dignity, individuality, and worth. Today you are
even more of a miracle because of the loss and self-sacrifice
you've been through.

Now, allow the dreams in your heart to rise. They were
placed there by God; woven into the fabric of your soul;
intended to be the very fire that drives and motivates you, filling your days with energy, happiness, and excitement. Pause
and thank God for the miracle of who you are. Let the wonder
of the real you begin to fill your heart.

In quiet, allow God's love to wash away any fears or misgiv-
ings you have about the future, because, in God, you are not
only a special creation—you have a destiny.

Designed for Destiny

There is more to your story than the fact that God knew you in the womb. Becoming the real you will also mean discovering the purpose for which He created you. In Jeremiah 1:4-5, we read:

> The word of the Lord came to me, saying, "Before I formed you in the womb I knew you, before you were born I set you apart; I appointed you as a prophet to the nations."

On the very dawn of Israel's exile into Babylon, Jeremiah was born with the unpopular and unpleasant destiny of the prophet's life. God destined him to be His voice during a most difficult time in Jewish history. That destiny came with unimaginable difficulty, and Jeremiah would need courage and strength.

The lives that you and I are called to will have their own challenges. Living an authentic life, giving place to our real self, will always require courage and strength. What God said to Jeremiah speaks to me personally. Through it I seem to hear God say, "Just as I knew Jeremiah, I knew you before you were conceived. And before you were born I had a plan for you. I have appointed you."

It took years for me to realize this truth: In God, nothing that happens to shape us is ever lost. Whether the people and events that molded us into the women we are now were positive or negative, in God's hands, they can be sculpting tools that shape us into the vessels of grace, compassion, generosity, vision, and spiritual greatness that He always intended.

It is my choice, and yours, whether or not what we experience will be surrendered to His purpose. Our lives, to this point, have been training camps for the women we can become. Only in recent years have I understood: When I let God use my formative experiences, something incredible happens. The pain I have experienced is transformed into a passion to protect and to heal. The wounding because of unfounded criticism has matured into a desire to hear real, constructive criticism—and even an ability to stand my ground in the face of wrongful criticism and confront the motives of the attacker! Because of my past, I have certain strengths I would not have otherwise.

What happened to many of us in the past was undoubtedly wrong and hurtful. It should not have happened. But it *did*. Now, it's up to us to choose whether or not the experiences will destroy, delay, or derail the real you and the real me.

I've made my choice. I have decided to use these experiences to make the real, authentic me stronger. I have chosen to let God use them to advance His work in me—and through me.

What about you? Have people, or circumstances, just about pressed the living dreams out of you? Do you define yourself by the heartaches and losses of your past, rather than by your future? Do you believe God can redeem your past, and use it to direct you into His appointed plan—actually fulfilling you beyond your farthest dreams?

Using your journal, why not revisit some of the hard experiences that have shaped who you are? Try to identify what part of your self was threatened. Referring to Jeremiah 1:4-5, how do you think your perception of those experiences would change if you heard God speak those same words to you?

Personal Reflection

In your notebook, address the following:

1. What do you know about the circumstances surrounding your conception? If you aren't sure (for example, if you were an adopted child), what do you know of your beginning in your childhood family circle?

2. Were there "forces" that just seemed set against you? Was it a struggle to survive?

3. As you grew up, what was encouraged? What was discouraged?

4. Did someone else always seem to have a plan for what you would do, what you would be? How did those plans differ from your own dreams or plans? When were you ever allowed the space to just be you?

5. Envision yourself in a past experience when you felt forced to turn aside from choices that were true to yourself. Write the experience in your journal.

Now, go a step beyond recalling the events: Let God whisper your name. Realize that He did not allow "deep waters" to sweep you entirely away, or allow the "fire" of pain-filled experiences to devour you. Let God love you … knowing that He loved you then, as He loves you now.

Prayerful Response

Dear Lord, let me see myself as You see me. Let me understand that while others may define some of my early experiences as teasing, I experienced them as torture. Help me value them as valid and valuable experiences, even if they represent pain. Where I couldn't, or didn't know to, trust You then, I choose to trust You now. I didn't know I could bring You into the painful situation then, but now I know I can invite You to go back to those wounded areas of my real me. Thank You, Lord, that I am a living example of someone You protected and brought through deep waters. Let the healing presence of Your Holy Spirit wash through my entire self, present and past. Amen.

Leaving the Real Me Behind

Can you imagine meeting someone for the very first time and having him know something about you that no one else could possibly know? It happened to Nathanael, a disciple of Jesus.

In John 1:45-49, we read that the apostle Philip eagerly searched for his friend Nathanael, and told him:

"We have found the one Moses wrote about in the Law, and about whom the prophets also wrote—Jesus of Nazareth, the son of Joseph."

"Nazareth! Can anything good come from there?" Nathanael asked. "Come and see," said Philip.

When Jesus saw Nathanael approaching, he said of him, "Here is a true Israelite, in whom there is nothing false."

"How do you know me?" Nathanael asked. Jesus answered,

"I saw you while you were still under the fig tree before Philip called you."

Then Nathanael declared, "Rabbi, you are the Son of God; you are the King of Israel."

What was Nathanael doing under the fig tree? What was he thinking and feeling? The Bible doesn't tell us, but Jesus knew without physically being there, and that convinced Nathanael that Jesus was indeed the long-awaited Messiah.

This verse spoke to me at a very deep level about the "fig tree" experiences of my early life—when God knew what experiences were shaping me, though I was unaware that He knew about me at all.

Even Then, He Saw Me ...

My mother knew something was wrong with me. I was withdrawing. Concerned, she arranged for me to attend school at the age of five. In our small community, there was a one-room schoolhouse for the first six grades. There was no kindergarten but, convinced I was smart enough to keep up, Mom sent me to school with one of my sisters and a cousin.

I was completely out of place. Instead of drawing me out socially, attending school caused me to withdraw even more. I coped by avoiding the other kids as much as possible, and lost myself in a favorite pastime: an imaginary play world in a corner of a large sandbox. I loved to feel the smooth, hot sand flowing between my fingers, and imagined it to be stardust sprinkled by fairies. I drew pictures and designs on the soft white surface with a stick. Left to my imaginary world, I was more than content.

One day I looked up from where I'd buried my feet in the warm, soft sand to discover the playground completely empty. I hadn't even heard the heavy cast-iron bell that called us inside. I was alone—and terrified.

My punishment was to stand in the coat closet. I wanted to die.

It happened again. This time, the schoolhouse door was locked. I had to pound with my fists. Inside, I faced laughter and jeering. My stomach churned with nausea. I spent the whole afternoon in shame, standing in the coat closet.

"You need to be more like the other children," I was lectured at home. I wanted to scream, *"But I'm not like them."* Instead, I agreed to try to be more like everyone else.

From then on, I tried very hard to get over my "overactive imagination and childish immaturity" (as my teacher termed it). Creativity and make-believe appeared to be my enemy, not my friend. I tried hard to pay attention, to listen, and to follow directions. I did exactly what I was told. Once in awhile I caught my mind drifting and I forced it back into regimented obedience and cooperation. The real me was not allowed in that classroom. The creative person inside had to sit in a corner inside me and be quiet.

Many years later, when I had elementary-aged children of my own, I came across the story of Nathanael's encounter with Christ. As I read the passage, God seemed to fit Jesus' words to my situation. "Just like I saw Nathanael under the fig tree, I saw you in the school yard." It was as if God were reassuring me, saying, *"I know you have a vivid imagination. I gave it to you! It's My gift to you, and I'd like you to use it for Me."*

I didn't know if I still *had* an imagination. For years I had fought being "a dreamer." The only time I ever let my creativity flow was if it was needed for church work or teaching a Sunday school class. Yet I wanted to serve God in any way I could, so—although I had no idea how hard it would be—I agreed to try.

What I took away from that experience was this: God has watched over every one of us, even when we have gone through experiences that have made us hide, or ignore our true selves in order to please someone else. He has been at work in us at these times, as He is at work in us now. And *now* He is asking that the dreams and drives He has woven into our very beings be given to Him for use in His great plan. For me, this has meant allowing Him to restore the creative, imaginative part of me I left behind in a sandbox in the California desert. He knew what had happened to the real me, and only He knew how to put me together again. He'll do the same for you.

Come Out of Hiding

Was there a time when you found it more advantageous *not* to be your real self? Can you remember when you chose to be something, or someone, other than yourself? Jesus wants you to know He saw you there. Long before this day, long before you even knew Him, He knew you.

Once I saw the personal message in Jesus' words to Nathanael, I knew what I had to do. I sat quietly in the Lord's presence. I allowed Him to reach back through my past and touch the wounds of rejection that had crippled my real self. That very day, I let Him begin to heal the little girl lost in her own thoughts and daydreams on the playground.

Will you let Him touch the experiences in you that lie buried and all but forgotten? Will you surrender to Him the times when you had to hide your true self from the eyes of others and begin to wear a pleasing mask?

Family Expectations

Only you can know why you began hiding your authentic self. There can be many reasons. Was there a sense of secret duty or obligation connected to your family? Susie knows what that's like. Her mother spent every day behind locked doors and drawn drapes. After school, when other little girls were outside playing jump rope or hopscotch, Susie was in the house looking after her mother.

"She had a nervous breakdown," Susie says. "At least that's what we were told to tell other people. The truth of it was that she usually started drinking before noon and by the time I got home from school she was nearly ready to pass out. She laid on the couch in front of the TV, watching the game shows every morning and the soaps every afternoon. My brother never came home from school until supper time. Dad would come home later on in the evenings. From the second grade on, I really took care of myself and made sure Mom didn't burn the house down with the forgotten cigarettes smoldering on the coffee table or in her bedroom. Sometimes she got sick..." Susie explains, twisting a tissue. "I had to clean it up."

Today, Susie hosts a backyard Bible club after school hours. "I want to reach those kids who feel like they're supposed to shoulder an adult-sized burden. Somehow I have an extra sense that allows me to spot those kids who are at risk. I know I can't save all the children, but I can make a difference in my own neighborhood."

Shame

Or do you remember a different kind of secret—an unbearable burden of shame—something you defined as so terrible you couldn't tell any other person? Marnie does. From the time she was a little girl. Her three older brothers weren't really very much company, and although her parents were loving and capable, she kept it secret when one of her brother's friends molested her. She was only four. "We'll both be in big trouble," he had warned.

Along with that shame, being the only girl around so many boys made her feel vulnerable. To protect herself, she developed an aggressive attitude. Eventually her tomboyishness became second nature; by the time she left for college she was questioning her sexuality. A lesbian rugby coach took an interest in her, and over the next few years she followed a pathway that led her farther and farther away from her true self. Even after accepting Christ, and with the help of supportive Christian friends, it took Marnie years of patient and persistent effort and personal responsibility to overcome the homosexuality for which she had set herself up with a four-year-old's decision.

These days, you will find Marnie involved in ministry helping others who have chosen to commit themselves to the terribly difficult inner work of overcoming homosexuality. "Unless you've been there," she says, "you can't even imagine the courage and inner strength this voyage to freedom requires. I want to offer others the same help and strength in Christ I found."

Not So Golden Rules

Some of us have lost our real selves because of severely enforced family or church rules. Even the simplest of expectations by the most well intentioned can make us veer off the course of life for which God created us. Some church cultures ignore the leadership, creative, or teaching abilities of women altogether. If a woman wants to serve God in these settings, she must take on a more "acceptable" role—allowing her true self to be driven into hiding. Family and church culture can dictate by defining a woman's choice of careers, husband, family size, and lifestyle—whether or not she likes the choices. That's when the real me goes into hiding.

Choices we have made to take our real me's into hiding are hard to unmake. Yet it is possible. Sarah is living proof. She didn't go into hiding willingly, and her undaunted spirit refused to let her stay there.

When Sarah's youngest child entered elementary school,

Sarah signed up for her first classes at her local community college. By the time the last of her children left home she had completed her course work in a nontraditional, external study Bible college. "I want to be a pastoral counselor," she says. "In addition to my education, I have a lot of life experiences to offer. I have already applied for ministerial credentials. Next year at this time I will be working in either a Christian counseling center or pastoral care and counseling at a church. Things have changed since I was younger—there are many more opportunities for women today. I plan to take every advantage of those changes."

Self-Imposed Exclusion

My friend Thea didn't know it, but she took her true self into hiding when she chose to become a stay-at-home mom to the exclusion of other interests. An elementary school teacher, she gladly gave up her position in education and gave herself entirely to her family and their needs. She home schooled, sponsored soccer teams, and planned exciting field trips and vacations that kept her little family together and happy.

Today, however, her youngest is in high school and planning to go off to college and a sad realization has finally hit. "While I gave myself to them, I didn't take care of *me*," she admits. "Now I almost have to begin again. I didn't keep up my teaching credentials, and now I have to decide all over again what I want to do with my life."

Thea would be the first one to tell you that the choices she made in the past—even though they were right at the time—were out of balance and have cost her something of her true self. Life changes, and her real me needs have changed too. She hasn't even considered, much less developed, other options. "I have to fight the feeling that I've fallen so far behind that I can't do anything about it now."

When we allow circumstances and roles to demand all our attention and energies, we may be setting ourselves on a long path away from personal fulfillment and satisfaction. Only when we stop filling empty spaces in our hearts and souls with others' expectations, deep, shame-filled secrets, cultural rules, and busyness can we begin to bring our true selves out into the open.

I abandoned my real me many times in my early years, but I will not do so anymore. I celebrate now what I left in the sand-box many years ago: I *am* creative and imaginative.

What have you left behind that deserves to be celebrated now? Why not take some time to be by yourself, and reclaim those parts of the real you that were left behind. Is there a gift or talent you abandoned because you were not given the opportunity to express or develop it? Even latent gifts are trea-sures of our real selves. Did you dream of being a painter or a poet, holding a political office, or owning a business? Write in your journal about those gifts and talents that remain dormant in you. Accept that part of the real you, and open your heart to it. Determine to let God love the entire person you are—the person you are inside.

In the previous chapter, we saw that people and circum-stances can cause us to give up our real selves. In this chapter, we have seen that God can use challenge and difficulty for His purposes. That's because God's plan of redemption is not launched outside our human condition, but within it.

Take some time to be alone before God and consider the following questions. What part of the real you was left behind? Was it an emotional need—like the desire to be loved and encouraged? Was it a talent? An ambition?

Are you afraid to accept that part of you now? Are you worried that it's "too late" for the real you to emerge and grow? Do you feel silly, or selfish, for wanting to pursue something you gave up a long time ago? It's important to be honest with yourself, because such ingrained attitudes will continue to sabotage you before you can grow and move forward.

Lastly, imagine yourself standing openhanded, openhearted before God. Quietly tell Him your dreams, your wants, and your desires. Allow Him to begin restoring the gift He intended to give you at the first—and let your true self emerge. He will not criticize what you are. He will not make you feel silly or ashamed. He made you.

If you will choose to walk with God like this, the adventure of a lifetime—your lifetime—can begin. Isn't this what you've wanted?

Personal Reflection

1. Do you have a "fig tree" experience? If God were to look back through your life and say to you personally, "I saw you, even then …," what do you think He'd refer to?

2. If God were to use the challenges and difficulties in your life that caused you to set aside your real me, how do you think He might do that?

3. How would your life change if you saw that He could not only help you reclaim your real me, but also put those experiences to work helping others to do the same? For example, would you help women about your age find their real me's too, or would you prefer to reach out to children of the same age you were when you set aside your real me?

4. List the hopes and dreams you have set aside as hopeless and unrealistic. Are they still hopeless and unrealistic? Why?

5. As you embrace your postponed inner dreams, how will you begin to adjust your life to include them?

Prayerful Response

Dear Father, help me learn how to overcome those obstacles that have prevented my real me from coming forward. Then help me to see how You can actually use those experiences for my good and for my development. I choose to embrace all that You've created me to be and to become my whole, real self. Amen.

THREE

How Do
I Get the
Real Me Back?

The reasons we have abandoned our real selves are as varied as human beings are.

Some of us have silenced our true selves out of fear—fear that we wouldn't be accepted, understood, or liked; fear that we couldn't withstand personal criticism. Some of us have been overly dependent on structure and rules that seem to tell us when we've measured up, living so that others know we're "good girls" all the time. We hang onto idealized images of what we "ought" to be. We agree to positions that are not our genuine point of view. And in all this, we surrender more pieces of our authentic self.

Living by Code

For far too many of us, being authentic runs against the "code" of Christian conduct we've learned. The code goes something like this: *Never* get angry (or at least never *show* anger), don't be too aggressive, don't insist on having your own way (even if you know you're dead right), and don't get too upset. *Always* be kind and considerate, automatically assume you've misunderstood when someone hurts your feelings, and always keep your demeanor soft.

For women, the subtle pressures that come to bear in a spiritual community can be great. There are pressures and unspoken rules about the way we dress, speak, and act; how we keep our homes and raise our children; and what work we can and can't do, both in church and in the working world. Christian women often consider it much safer to conform, especially in more rigid and rule-bound Christian circles, choosing *uniformity* over *authenticity*.

Is this what God wants? *In order to be Christians, do we have to resort to a false sameness—giving up genuine emotion, personal opinions, creative thought, and individual uniqueness?*

Think about it: When was the last time you withheld an opinion or an idea because you were afraid it might be misinterpreted, misunderstood, or rejected entirely? Didn't you sense you were somehow letting yourself down? Have you suppressed your desire to seek a position because you might look too aggressive, or too eager, if you pursued it? Or—more common, perhaps—have you taken on a volunteer task, knowing full well your schedule was full? Are you driven by guilt to say yes when you should say no?

We have abandoned our real selves in too many ways. Now it's time to find the authentic you, and begin to grow into beautiful maturity.

How does a woman *find* her real self?

Searching Your Heart

"I lost part of myself when I decided to be strong and not be sad when my father died," says Lori. "I gave up a piece of me when I had breast implants to please my husband," says Jilene. "I betrayed myself when I didn't try for a promotion at work," says Carla, "because I didn't want to be seen as ambitious." "I give up my self when I let my family run my day ... and my *life*," says Jeri, the mother of teenagers.

"To be honest, I feel guilty admitting I feel empty and incomplete," Marlane says. "After all, I'm a Christian. Wasn't Christ supposed to make me 'whole' when I gave my life to God?"

Like Marlane, you may need to correct a wrong belief that seems to hold back many Christians. Many of us were taught that when a person accepts Christ, that person becomes a new creation. It's true that something vital changes instantly the moment we come to Christ. Our spiritual new birth provides forgiveness of our sins, hope for the future, and access to our heavenly Father. We are given a clean slate—a brand new beginning.

But becoming a Christian doesn't automatically restore our

true selves, or reestablish our personal authenticity. It isn't a guarantee that we'll stop giving our real selves away inappropriately. Being in fellowship with God, however, does give us the strength, courage, and even motivation to become the women we were created to be. In fact, accepting Christ is the first all-important step toward inner wholeness.

Many people understand and know Christ as their Savior, and even have a grasp on what it means that He redeemed them from sin. But many never *experience* His full redemption in the area of reclaiming their true, whole selves. Yes, being redeemed from the penalty of sin is more wonderful than we can understand. But the redemptive process includes becoming whole—that is, reclaiming parts of our selves that have been abandoned and scattered.

Personal reclamation takes work—the work of cooperating with God, and obeying Him, as He brings our authentic selves to light, so we can reclaim the lives He intended for us. To be perfectly honest, this is often hard work. Perhaps this is where we Christians make our mistake. Though it's true we can do nothing to earn our salvation, we think that God's healing gifts of grace require no effort on our part. Nothing is further from the truth.

One of the hardest pieces of work we have to do is to *be honest* about who we are, what we think, and what we want. I believe the psalmist knew how hard this kind of honesty before God is when he wrote:

O Lord, you have searched me and you know me. You know when I sit and when I rise; you perceive my thoughts from afar. You discern my going out and my lying down; you are familiar with all my ways. Before a word is on my tongue you know it completely, O Lord.

PSALM 139:1-4

Jeremiah may have understood this, too, when he wrote:

You know me, O Lord; you see me and test my thoughts about you.

JEREMIAH 12:3

It takes a great deal of spiritual work—coupled with courage and trust in the love of God—to open ourselves before Him like this. Where can you and I find the courage to experience the redemption, the reclaiming, of our true selves?

Opportunity for a Miracle

Maybe you've been a "pleaser" too long. Maybe you've sacrificed yourself for your children, for your husband, or because you've been living by "rules" that have told you what you can and can't be. Maybe some of you have been so constantly put down that you've come to believe your real selves are of little value. Whatever the case, you need to begin to stand on this truth: *You were born with value and promise, a bundle of potential.*

Knowing this and taking back the ground that's been lost are entirely different matters.

I've already mentioned the first step toward reclaiming your true self—giving your heart anew to Jesus Christ, to let Him redeem your soul and your life. How amazing that the One who created the universe wants to be involved in our lives! Amazing that no matter how unlovely or worthless we might feel, He loves us beyond what we can imagine.

Stop and consider this more closely. Through a simple prayer of repentance and surrender to Jesus Christ, God comes close to us, without hesitation. And the Bible says that there is nothing for which He will even scold or blame us (see Col 1:21-23). He comes with the gift of eternal life in His hands, and unconditional love in His heart. All He wants is to offer a divine friendship, sweet and pure, unlike any relationship we've known before. As we surrender more and more of our lives to Him, embrace His love, and seek His will, He begins to work yet another miracle: *He begins to create the real person within—the person He had in mind from the beginning.* This is a miracle that no amount of abuse, stalling, failure, sin, disappointment, neglect, or personal tragedy can hold back!

Now we're faced with the opportunity for a miracle—the chance to become our real, God-intended selves. True, this will take our cooperation, as we saw earlier. But we can escape the frustration, the trap of pleasing others at the expense of ourselves, the pretense, the false impressions we have worked so hard to create. Talents once denied can spring to life anew. Personality and inner beauty can blossom. The wholeness of God is now available. This is the life Jesus promised when He said, "The thief comes only to steal and kill and destroy; I have come that they may have life, and have it to the full" (Jn 10:10).

It's up to us to make room in our lives to accommodate what God offers. Will you do this? Will you have the courage and take the chance to be all God intended you to be?

In your journal, you may want write about the areas where you want or need to become the real you. Write out any reservations you may have about letting God into your life at this level. For instance, Vicki confides that she is afraid God will think her goals and ideas are stupid or trivial. Anya is concerned that if she begins to use her strengths and talents, her husband will feel very threatened.

You may want to write about the changes that will have to take place if you let God begin to reveal the real you. What inner changes do you want to make? Phoebe wants to stop telling herself that "my husband and children are all that matter," and begin to make a little space in her life for her own dreams and talents. Jen wants to stop being so self-critical, and to allow herself to learn and grow in her decorating skills.

Perhaps you've never thought of it before, but these are important life issues. God wants you to make them a matter of prayer. *Talk with Him about what goes on in your head. Let Him point out thoughts and wrong beliefs that undermine the strength you need to become your true self.*

This is where your cooperation comes in.

Solitude

To carry on this kind of important dialogue with God, you will have to make space in your life. You will need "alone time" with Him. I can hear you protest—"My life is too hectic!" In the Bible, we see Jesus in constant contact with people, at such depths and in such numbers that it had to be physically exhausting. No one understands the demands on your time and energy like He does. But He made His way to quiet mountainsides to be alone with God, and His example shows us the importance of learning to be still and undistracted so that God can respond. Consider the high priority Jesus placed on "alone time" with God:

> After he had dismissed [the multitude], he went up on a mountainside by himself to pray. When evening came, he was there alone....
>
> MATTHEW 14:23

> Jesus left there and went along the Sea of Galilee. Then he went up on a mountainside and sat down.
>
> MATTHEW 15:29

In both of these scriptures, Jesus is hungry for solitude. Sometimes He went off alone to pray (see Lk 22:41). Sometimes it seems He just needed to be by Himself. When was the last time you just got off somewhere, or shut the door and left the world and all its cares outside? How many times have you felt that the pace of your life was sapping your strength and robbing you of time to reflect and pray? We need more than sleep to replenish emotional and physical strength. We need time to be alone with our thoughts and feelings before a loving God who wants to quiet, sort out, and direct our soul.

I'll be the first to admit that finding time for myself is hard. At this stage of my life, all my children are grown and living away from home. You'd think solitude would come easier. But the truth is this: Yes, I'm an early riser and have hours to myself every day; yes, I work in a small, quiet office away from the house; and yes, I'm totally alone most days—but I still find that quiet personal reflection is an inner struggle. For one thing, it's easy to fall back into old routines of having to produce. For another, facing internal struggles honestly means I might see what I'm doing wrong, if anything, or changes I need to make in my life—and change is difficult. Finally, just resting, and being *me* before God? Sounds selfish, doesn't it?

How do we overcome the life conditioning that keeps us from the rejuvenating time with God we need? Personally, I have to discipline myself to spend time in solitude. I make myself understand that, just as a good night's sleep regenerates my body, solitude regenerates my mind and spirit. Solitude takes me out of life's "fray" so I can gain the strength to return to the pace and extend myself to those who need and depend on me.

Frankly, it took a long time to come to terms with my need for solitude with God. I didn't come to it easily. But remembering these few truths helps:

Being alone is not the same as being lonely.
I'm a "people person" by nature. I relate well to strangers, meet new people with ease, and enjoy being with friends and family. Cutting myself off from people, even for brief periods, often seemed gloomy and lonely—until I learned that solitude

doesn't have to mean loneliness. It just means I'm alone with God and me!

Seeking solitude doesn't mean you're odd or eccentric.
Anyone can find biographies of great scholars, artists, and writers who spent inordinate periods of time alone in what could be defined by most as a particular and individualistic type of pursuit. But everyday people also need time alone to form opinions, identify feelings, clarify convictions, and make decisions.

Those who seek solitude can function well in the everyday world.
Those of us who have braved the challenges of maintaining the discipline of periodic solitude often find we actually function better in the demands of work, church, and home because of time spent alone. Those of us who absolutely need solitude know that we do not function well in our daily routine without it.

For me, real stability comes from my times of solitude. I become more sure of myself, my point of view, and my decisions. I'm less likely to make a rash decision or do something against my best interest if I have given myself some solitude and thinking room.

Solitude is not my way of escaping from the pain or stress of the real world.
In fact, solitude is really an effective way of dealing with both the stress and painful situations of everyday life. In solitude I find it easier to quietly stretch my faith, to gather the strength

to trust God a little further and hold on longer. I'm not withdrawing in any sense other than for the purpose of reentry as a stronger, calmer, quieter person.

In solitude I gain tremendous spiritual insight.

Bible study and prayer are invaluable and essential, but it's not in either of those activities that I gain the insights to Scripture I need to face the challenges of my life and ministry. I truly feel as if I have cheated myself if after I read the Bible and pray, I don't spend a few extra minutes in quiet aloneness before God. Not really praying, not even meditating, just "steeping"— simply *being*.

Solitude gives me the opportunity to see my own challenges and troubles from an entirely different perspective.

I don't know about you, but sometimes I am too close to my own problems to see them, or their possible solutions, clearly. Taking a step away—actually, physically closing a door against my world of responsibility and relationships—gives me a sense of healthy distance, a safe emotional balcony from which to look down at my life and see things as a whole.

Solitude is where I discover the strength to make changes and to take paths dictated by my heartfelt convictions.

It's so easy to let myself be needed by so many that I end up abandoning my own pressing needs. Or to make judgments based on expectations rather than on truly deep-seated convictions. Solitude helps me remain true to myself—the person inside.

Solitude encourages my reflective side and my imaginative, creative gifts.

My writing isn't done at the computer keyboard. It's created in solitude. This book wasn't formed with a dictionary in one hand and a Bible in the other—it came out of my solitary moments.

Solitude gives me the opportunity to better know and accept myself.

More than once I've taken a hurtful accusation into my solitude and simply asked myself, *Is that true?* Whether it's a conflict with a friend who thinks I'm less than thoughtful, a church administrator who thinks I should give more time and energy, or the unrealistic expectations of family, I am more likely to recognize the truth if I give myself time alone to process. When the popular opinion runs against my grain, or the usual "Christian" role or rule doesn't quite fit my situation, it's in solitude that I come to resolution and peace.

Answers Out of Silence

In light of what we've just learned about solitude and some of the myths we've now replaced with the truth, let yourself think about the following questions:

Do I avoid being alone because I'm afraid of being lonely?

Does taking time away from family and friends make me feel odd or eccentric?

What responsibilities or demands of work, church, and

home could possibly benefit if I took some time alone?

Perhaps it's time you learned to spend some time in solitude. You'll be surprised how much even a few minutes of solitude will change you and the way you approach and handle the pressures of your life. Try it for just three or four days in a row. You don't need hours. You can find solitude in minutes, if that's all you can manage.

Each time you experience solitude, use the last five minutes to write in your journal. Record your feelings and note any struggle you had in giving yourself these moments of solitude. What hindrances did you encounter? What can you do to increase your solitude time? What determined when your alone time ended?

Just to "Be"

Is it awkward for you just to *be*, rather than *do*? For many women, it is.

But if you can once capture the freedom that comes from *being* a chosen, cherished child of God rather than *doing* the Christian life, record it as a spiritual "Kodak moment." In your mind and heart freeze-frame the experience. When you do, you'll begin to transform into your real self at last. Here is where you actually begin to become the real person God desired and designed. No one, no experience, no haunting memory or personal failure will ever be able to take that from you again.

Making a space in your life to meet with God in solitude is

an important discipline to bring into your life. Next, we'll take a look at how to get the most personal growth from solitude.

Personal Reflection

1. What are some of your biggest obstacles to finding time for solitude? How can you overcome them or adjust your life to accommodate the discipline of solitude?
2. If you were to give yourself permission to go away for the weekend all by yourself, where would you go, and what would you do?
3. If you had someone else to cook dinner for you once in a while, how would you use the extra time?
4. When someone asks you to take on one more task when you know your schedule is already full, how can you make sure you're not making a mistake by saying no—or even yes?
5. After reading this chapter, what practical considerations concerning solitude occur to you?

Prayerful Response

Dear Father, I choose to come into Your presence alone and with a quieted heart. I wait before You and bring my hopes, dreams, and ideas to be exposed to Your love and grace. For these few moments I set aside self-criticism, self-doubt, and self-made opinions. I choose to simply be here with You, open and vulnerable to Your love. Amen.

FOUR

In the
Company
of One

"What goes on in the human being when he is by him-self is as important as what happens in his interac-tions with other people," says Anthony Storr, author of *Solitude*.[1]

Many of us want what solitude can give us: peace and a return to a sense of being "centered" and "on-balance." But solitude itself is daunting. When we're alone, we can become uncomfortable. Given a day off, we begin to cram it full again. Left on our own for even an hour, we reach for the TV remote, or the radio. The truth is, being alone, with ourselves or with God, is too much for many of us. Yet we sense that spiritual maturity, inner health—maybe even physical health, and surely our real self—lie on the other side of quiet and solitude.

How can we get the most out of what limited time we have to devote to this wonderful and self-renewing discipline?

Are You Willing to be an "Original"?

Like most of us, you may find that taking even a few minutes for yourself can be nearly impossible. Solitude does not promise us the same rewards that the company of friends does. The rewards of being alone are not instant, like those of chatting over coffee; they are longer in coming. The personal growth and inner balance that allow the real you to emerge are a *lifetime achievement*. To become your authentic self takes time. If you, like me, are looking forward to growth and development from now on, be prepared: it will take your entire lifetime. Delayed reward and gratification are a bit foreign to those of us who are used to getting *what* we want, *when* we want it. We would rather be like the cheap lithograph print, which takes seconds to reproduce, than like the original masterpiece, which cost the artist her whole life to create.

We begin to be an "original," a true work of art, authentic and from the hand of God, when we set aside just a few minutes and *invest ourselves* in becoming what God has designed us to be. He has the blueprint; we have the time.

A Map Through Solitude

Let's explore together ways to make the most of your alone time. As we do, it may be helpful to note in your journal practical ways you can apply these suggestions in your own situation.

Dedicate your alone time to personal inner growth and regenerative activities.

People pay hundreds and thousands of dollars to therapists to learn what I'm about to tell you here and now: *You are the only one who can take the responsibility for your inner growth and health.*

I spoke to a young woman who had been severely abused and molested as a young girl. After she told me her story, she sobbed, "I can't forgive him!"

Who could blame you? I thought. Thankfully, I prayed for wisdom before I responded. While what was done to her was a terrible crime, it can be damaging to encourage bitterness. As I prayed, I saw that the main block to her healing was this very thing—*forgiveness.* I saw that the need to punish and repay had taken hold, and her spirit was consumed with thoughts of hate and revenge, spilling over in mistrust and misplaced anger even in her good relationships.

"Every time I go for prayer, people tell me I should just simply forgive him. But what he did to me was unforgivable!"

"I understand," I said, then took a deep breath and prayed for strength and the right words. "So don't forgive him. At least not now."

She was shocked. I know she was expecting the usual Christian litany.

"You didn't deserve what happened to you," I plunged in. "It's unthinkable and cruel. But you don't deserve to live your life with *unforgiveness*—all the hatred and bitterness—eating at your soul either, do you?"

She considered.

"So forget about forgiving *him*. Let's deal with the unforgiveness that will devour *you*."

For some time, we discussed possible ways of getting rid of the unforgiveness, hatred, and bitterness. Eventually, together we arrived at the same conclusion: She could only confess and surrender these emotions to God.

Then I guided her into a time of quiet prayer. This was not exactly pure solitude, since I was in her company. But it was the first step of solitude, in which I helped her to stop thinking about other people and what they did to her, and instead to consider herself—that is, the condition of her soul. Fortunately, she followed beautifully. In prayer, she confessed these destructive emotions, and asked God to forgive her for carrying them for nearly twenty years. Then she asked to be released from them, and began to lay each emotion at the foot of the cross by simply surrendering it to God. She asked that the forgiving, cleansing blood of Jesus cover her sins, and poured out her desire to be free from the whole situation that had seethed within her, poisoning and controlling so many years of her young life.

What happened that day was the kind of miracle that happens when we are taught how to meet ourselves in solitude. This beautiful young woman was now taking responsibility for her inner life and spiritual health. She couldn't change the despicable things that had happened to her, but she could keep them from damaging her further. She could stop her past from stealing from her present and casting a distorting shadow over her future. At the same time, she began to deepen in her relationship with her heavenly Father, the only One strong enough to bear all the burdens we can't.

What about you? Are there destructive and damaging emotions within your inner self keeping you from engaging fully in rich and meaningful relationships with others, with life, with yourself, and even with God?

Determine that you will get alone and take the time and responsibility to feed your own soul.

For too long we've handed over the responsibility for our own spiritual nourishment to others. We depend on someone else to come up with answers to our hard questions about life, rather than growing strong by groping for answers ourselves. We wait for people to offer words of affirmation or approval. We hope for gestures of thoughtfulness. We may even pump and manipulate others for indications of our worth. Whenever we give in to this impulse to "be fed," we do so because we haven't taken the responsibility for our own spiritual care and inner nourishment. To leave this in the hands of others is to set yourself up for a lifetime of dependence—and disappointment.

It's time to determine that this attempt to draw your sense of well-being from others is done. Learning to be alone in our good company doesn't mean we spend our alone time puffing ourselves up with superficial compliments; it means that we begin to learn what it is that nourishes our own souls.

I'll cover the more practical elements of this in a later chapter, but for now, take a moment to determine who you have depended on up to now for your sense of well-being.

Be honest with yourself about the following:

I have depended on (husband, children, friends, or _____) for emotional nourishment and spiritual feeding.

If I began to take the responsibility myself, it would certainly change the way I ...

I know that I feed and nourish my own inner self when I ...

Dedicate some of your alone time to reflection and contemplation.

Sorting out life's questions and arriving at a personal position can be hard work. Think about it. Even watching your favorite sitcom, laugh tracks decide for you if something is funny or not. During election season, political candidates try to tell us what to think, what we want, and what is best for us. Well-meaning spouses often tell us what we should or shouldn't think, and whether we should or shouldn't feel a certain way. An employer can decide whether we're doing an acceptable job, and a grade on a term paper indicates whether we're making the grade intellectually.

Our worth, and our true self, does not have to depend on such outer approval. Simply being by yourself will give you the chance to form your own opinions. It can help you decide if your effort is the best it can be, and whether you should give beyond your present level in relationships, work, or at church. Only through the effort of reflection on our own lives can we accurately assess whether we're living up to our own potential, meeting our own standards, and growing into the real people God designed us to be.

Devote some times of solitude to deeper prayer experiences that go beyond praise, worship, thanksgiving, or petition to purposely, silently, quietly experiencing God, not just prayer.

Just because we pray, it doesn't mean we have experienced *God*. Prayer is when we stretch our faith and verbal expressions to reach toward Him. Contemplative prayer times are those precious times when we sit in open, uncluttered receptivity, inviting God to reach to us. In silence and waiting, we let the embrace of heaven encompass all of our earthly selves. We allow God to bathe us in His unconditional love. We let our souls breathe eternity in the here and now.

Investing in Yourself

As you can see, devoting some portion of our busy lives to solitude isn't the same as napping or staring off into space. It can be exciting, growth producing, and strengthening. It can deepen our relationship with Christ, and move us along toward discovering His specific will for our lives—not just our outer *doings*, but our inner *beings*. It is an investment in becoming authentic from the core.

Are there other things we can do to make sure we get the most out of solitude? Consider these important investments in your growth as a whole person:

Alone time is when we can explore the beliefs we hold, not only about God, but also ourselves. KerryAnne believed that, because of a gross failure in her past, she would always be a "second-class citizen" in God's kingdom. Because of that, she didn't believe He really heard her prayers … and because of that, she lived with the constant anxiety that something terrible would happen to her children, and God would ignore her pleas for mercy and help. The result of all this was that she perpetually "performed" as a Christian, trying to "make it up" to God in hopes she might catch His attention and win His love. There was absolutely no space or time to relax, experience freedom, and become her true self. She was way too busy working at being, in her words, "Mrs. Perfect Christian." Confronting all these layers of wrongly based thinking took a great deal of time in silence and solitude, but the investment in her own freedom from misbeliefs was worth every second.

Alone time can also help us to identify simple negative beliefs we may hold about ourselves, and to recognize where they come from. It was in quietness that Shelley finally recognized the voice that told her she was too stupid to get the kind of career breaks she hoped for—a voice that held her back from even trying. In prayer one day, God seemed to bring back the memory of a high school teacher, who had held her up to the whole class as "the prime example of a poor student who will never achieve anything in life"—both embarrassing her and utterly destroying her confidence.

When we identify wrong beliefs and negative influences, we can begin to heal their evil influences in our lives. Memories that have caused us to think or believe shameful and awful things about ourselves can be laid aside in light of God's love and mercy. We turn in a new direction, with new strength, when we begin to reassure ourselves, instead, that through

Christ we have a purpose and a destiny.

Once we release ourselves from prisons of the past, something truly great begins to happen. When we're willing to do the inner work solitude allows, we find the strength to think and dream beyond current limitations. When we dare to be alone and experience God's loving presence, we finally begin to realize the wonderful truth not only about Him, but also about ourselves. Perhaps for the first time, we know we are the loved and valued children of almighty God.

Solitude—standing alone before God—is what teaches us that we were each created to be distinct and different from anyone else. What a reward from so little an investment. For just a moment we detach from the world, and we begin to understand what it means to be destined for good and lovely things in God's kingdom. We begin to know by experience what it means to live the life of those separated, set apart for fellowship with His Majesty. We can finally allow ourselves the freedom to be *in* the world but no longer *of* it.

A New You

Actually, this kind of spiritual growth is known by another, biblical, term. It is the inner work of regeneration that we experience through solitude. It's surrendering what God truly created in you back into His hands, free of the soul-weakening, soul-sickening demands others have placed upon you. It is the process of renewal and restoration. And it happens when we pull away routinely and allow God the space to show us the ungodly influences that have shaped us ... against the shape of the true selves He originally created us to be.

So, it is through a holy self-examination that we experience true blessing—that is, a state of peace, in which we can accept ourselves. In the end, we may even arrive at that much-needed gift of *self-trust*—that place where we finally are guided by our own drives and instincts, knowing they were placed within us by God. In essence, we learn that all our lives are lived in the presence of God, and so we let Him love us deeply, discovering in the process that we can also love ourselves. For the Christian alone, this is where self-discovery leads.

Now we can begin to realize not only what happened to the real me in each of us, but also how to get her back ... for good.

Practically Speaking

You and I both know that, wonderful as this sounds, living an authentic life, drawing strength from solitude and quiet before God, is a huge challenge. Practically speaking, we have families, friends, and responsibilities. Every morning, life waits at the door. This is where commitment to God, and to yourself, must take over.

The most wonderful thing solitude gives me is the strength to face and cope with whatever awaits me upon my return. When I faithfully maintain a discipline of regularly attending to my inner self through solitude, I discover the inner peace and strength I need to handle the pressures of my life. My inner self is intact and my direction seems clearer. I'm more focused and able to maintain a strong faith in the face of difficulty.

Recently, my regular routine of solitary moments was interupted by one family crisis after another. My prayer time and Bible reading became perfunctory and dry. My feelings were easily hurt and old wounds began to resurface. I found myself questioning God. Doubt crept in around the edges of my relationship with Him. I began to wonder again about my future and worry about my usefulness to Him. In short, I was slipping back into old patterns of self-centeredness as a result of self-neglect. I wasn't any good to anyone—least of all to me! Once I took time to withdraw, however—to detach myself through solitude and engage in more contemplative prayer—I began to see what had happened to erode me at the core. I'd let the needs of others supersede my responsibility to feed and nourish my own soul.

Once again, I understood that my ministry to others could not happen without first tending to my own inner needs. That real ministry only happens through my life when my inner person is whole, nourished, and well fed. Disciplining my life in order to make room for solitude helps me do that.

How about you?

Are you ready to learn how to live from a soul that is centered in quiet and peace, strong enough to take on the rest of life? More of the real you waits to be discovered, as we now step back to get a fuller picture of your life.

Personal Reflection

Use these incomplete sentences as a springboard to help you learn more. Write without editing or limiting yourself. Let your real self express your deepest thoughts and desires about experiencing God's love.

1. The hardest thing I have ever had to get past is ...

2. The most difficult emotion for me to manage is ...

3. I have depended on (husband, children, friends, or _____) for emotional nourishment and spiritual feeding.

4. If I began to take the responsibility myself it would certainly change the way I ...

5. I know that I feed and nourish my own inner self when I ...

6. I want to give myself permission and enough credit to make up my own mind about ...

7. If I were to decide more for myself what I think and feel—even believe—it would mean that ...

8. When I let God love me at this level I ...

9. To experience God means to me that ...

Prayerful Response

Dear Father, I come into Your presence now, not to ask, not to get or do anything except to be alone with You. I long to let Your love seep deep into my parched soul, to experience You and let the hungers of my heart be met here in this place. Thank You, Father, that You know me, opinions, weaknesses, strengths, mis-beliefs, and all, and yet, You love me. Help me to know You better. Amen.

FIVE

Making Time for the Real Me

L ose your keys and you can't start your car. Lose your checkbook and your shopping trip is a total waste. Lose your map and you can lose your way. Lose your inner self, what I call the "real me," and you lose a very real part of your purpose, your destiny, and God's plan for your life.

Making the time to let your true self emerge is the challenge. As you know by now, many are discovering that solitude is a key. In reality, however, many of us wonder where in the world we can find even fifteen or twenty minutes to be alone.

Recovering Lost Treasure—You

The first step is to have a firm conviction that finding your true self is one of the most valuable things you can do. Better than finding lost treasure. If you are truly tired of dancing to tunes you no longer care about, you will do anything to find the authentic self God created.

The second step is a willingness to discipline yourself to make the time you need—what I call the outer work. Let's begin this process together, with a simple assessment of your life and relationships as they are currently.

Each of the following statements gives you food for thought. As you write your response to each statement in your journal, ask the Holy Spirit to help make the following identifications:

Identify the season of life that you are living.
The Bible says, "There is a time for everything, and a season for every activity under heaven ..." (Eccl 3:1). Our lives are seasonal. Any woman past forty has only to reflect on her life to recognize the truth of this passage.

Recently my mom went to live in an assisted living center. She occupies one-half of a moderately sized room. She has a bed, a dresser, and a chair. Through the years I've watched her sort her collected belongings, portion out her keepsakes, give away family pictures, and disburse mementos. My observation is that each time she has moved, first from a house to an apartment, then to a smaller mobile home, and now to her half-a-room, she's gone through a "distillation" process. Everything she owns is brought out and handled gently, and memories surface. The few things she still holds dear are what you might call the "pure essence" of her life and loves. She has lovingly parted with things that no longer fit into the current season of her life.

This is what each one of us must do in a spiritual sense, as well, because the changing seasons of a woman's life help her determine how to make room for the solitude she needs in order to grow.

For example, if you're recently married, you know the demands of adjusting and the added responsibilities of creating a home and a loving relationship. If you have a five-year-old on a half-day kindergarten schedule, you may have mornings or afternoons to choose from. If you're caring for toddler twins, you won't. If your teenagers are in school and driving themselves to and from all their activities, the demands on your time are different. If you're a widow, you know the sudden impact of deafening silence and the release from having to cook daily meals.

Depending on the season of your life, you may find yourself trying to capture even a moment to be alone, or searching for things to fill an empty day.

Where can you find the time to spend in solitude?

Meditate on Ecclesiastes 3:1-8, and consider its sweeping wisdom about the seasons of life. Spend time reflecting on your own life. Take into consideration your age, the changes you have already made in your life, and the changes you anticipate ahead. Try to identify the season of your life right now. Are you in the springtime, full of promise and new growth? In the summer, full of sunlight and plans and activity? In the fall, ready to gather in a full and bountiful harvest? In the winter, a time of rest and reflection?

Identify the roles you presently fill.
Mother, wife, friend, sister, daughter, housekeeper, secretary, breadwinner, chauffeur, nurse, tutor, crisis manager, grocery shopper … need I go on? The list can be absolutely endless.

Just as the seasons in our lives change, so do our roles. To find, make, or take time for solitude, many have had to be creative in working around their many roles and the time requirements involved.

Time for Yourself—Then for Others

Identify those who have a legitimate claim to your time.
In your journal, make a list of your family, or those with whom you live, and any close friends who lay claim to your time and your energy. Now, give them each a rating, not in order of importance or even perceived biblical priority, but in order of how much of your time their legitimate needs require. In other words, don't give your husband a higher priority rating if in reality you're giving higher priority to your children or your career. For some of us, it may now begin to come clear why we haven't done the hard work to find the time to be alone before. We have no time to give ourselves.

Now, look at the list again. How much time do the people in your life *really* require? I have used the word *legitimate* twice. Go over the list with that word firmly in mind. Is their need actually *legitimate*? If so, is it a legitimate use of *your* time? In other words, are there legitimate needs on your list that certainly need to be met, but could just as easily be met by someone else? For example, could you carpool instead of driving the kids yourself every day? Could you arrange for another neighbor to take the lady across the street to the mall or to the doctor? Could you arrange to co-chair a committee, splitting the work and responsibility? Could you delegate more household chores to the kids? Could you say no to the heart association or church fund-raiser this year? What I'm suggesting is that you begin to question whether *you* are really needed, or whether *anyone* would do.

When you made your list, did you put your own name there? Aren't you involved in your own life, too? Don't your needs deserve to be considered legitimate as well? How can you take the pressure off yourself in order to give you more of the time you need for personal development?

Would better organization in the evening save you precious minutes the next morning? Could you wait quietly in the car during your child's piano lesson, instead of running errands? Could you order winter jackets from a catalog instead of dragging everyone to the mall? Could you make several meals at one time, freeze them, and give yourself an extra hour or two later on in the week?

I want to encourage you to begin to make whatever efforts you must to push back the avalanche of demands on you and your time, in order to make space in your life to be alone with God. As your soul has longed to be free and filled, He has longed for you.

Consider Jesus' words from Matthew 23:37: "How often I have longed to gather your children together, as a hen gathers her chicks under her wings, but you were not willing."

Meditate on this statement. How can we find such a place under the wings of the Almighty? If you could hear God speaking this verse directly to you, what would be your response? That would be a good thing to write about in your journal.

Identify the "should's" and "shouldn'ts"—the unspoken rules—by which you govern your life.
Whether we admit it or not, the roles and relationships in our lives often come with their own set of rules. Sometimes these are based on faulty values and perceptions of what is acceptable, or even required in order to be a "good" mom, sister, wife, friend, or whatever.

It's so easy to fall into the trap of believing we should never say "no" to someone we really care about. It's easy to feel that the "Christian" thing to do is to always put others before ourselves. Let's take a closer look at what the Bible *really* says about this? One of the most famous passages on which Christian behavior is based is found in Philippians 2:1-13. Buried within that passage is what I call the "only-also" principle, which on first glance seems to tell us to ignore our own needs:

> Each of you should look not only to your own interests, but also to the interests of others. (v. 4)

Many of us need to look long and hard at this passage. Considering our overcrowded, overfilled calendars and overcommitted schedules, this verse might as well read, "Each of you should look not to your own interests, but *only* to the interests of others." But it doesn't, does it? Instead, it acknowledges that we each have needs we must attend to … before we look to the needs of other people. "Each of you should look *not only to your own interests*"—there it is. The basic assumption that we *are* taking care of ourselves.

Most of us take great pains to make sure we accommodate the needs of others. Some of us give in to their demands, too. Add to that the expectations of a Christian subculture and we are fried. Soon our lives operate according to the should's and shouldn'ts foisted on us by roles, relationships, and subsequent unquestioned rules, and we are way out of harmony with the wholeness God speaks of in the Bible.

I strongly suggest you read Philippians 2:1-13 for yourself. It is a marvelous passage that speaks of the way Jesus emptied Himself in order to fulfill His part in the work of God. But as you read, I want you to notice, and underline, the phrases that speak of Jesus' servanthood. For Jesus lived in obedience to *God*, not in subservience to *people*. It was out of obedience to God that His servanthood to mankind was even possible. His strong relationship with the heavenly Father gave Him the strength to manage the constant press of people.

And in the midst of it all, we know that Jesus sought solitude. He was a servant to people, yes, but not in every waking minute of every day of His life. He had the wisdom to get away—even from those He was committed to serve.

From the Philippians passage, you may find it helpful to list phrases that speak to you about serving others. Ask yourself: *would spending a little time in solitude really keep me from doing that?* Then think about it from another perspective and ask: *could spending time alone help me to better be God's servant in the lives of others?*

Identify your need for approval.

Living to please others is very common, and it's even thought to be admirable. Most of us don't want to make anyone mad, let anyone down, or cause anyone distress. We make choices that are good for others, but not for our authentic selves. We're good to everyone else, but not good to ourselves. Driven by our need for approval, our lives are taken over by others. All this is to the detriment, and sometimes the demise, of our true inner being.

I am a perfect case in point. I love peace. I can't stand tension in relationships, and in the past I thought no price was too high to pay for serenity and calmness in my home and friendships. Even groveling was not too high a price to pay, if peace could be maintained. Needless to say, there were many times I swallowed my own opinion, gave up my personal perspective, and even denied my own real feelings, just to maintain peace.

It took me many years to accept the fact that instead of growing, I had become a pleaser in the interest of keeping peace. Even some of my most personal and important relationships still bear the scars and are bound by years of my acquiescence when what the relationship really called for was the assertion of my strength. My self-respect was damaged and my self-confidence annihilated on more than one important occasion.

As you can guess, as a result of not wanting to cause trouble, I've worked for less pay, given in when I was right, and kept my mouth shut when I should have spoken out. In my own view, because I gave in to the immediate desire for peace at any price, I paid the ultimate price. I betrayed my own, true, inner self.

All because I didn't take the time, or make the effort, to challenge myself to grow. Unfortunately, it was many years before I discovered what I was doing. I was serving others, yes, but *in place of,* not *out of,* my real self.

Giving into my fear of encountering rough moments in relationships fed my need for approval, but I did not grow into a well-balanced, whole person. I became a peacekeeper instead of a peacemaker. And I sabotaged my real me many times in the process. Have you ever heard it said of someone, "She shot herself in the foot?" That's me. Crippled by my own need for approval.

How about you? How much approval, and whose, do you need? What have you given up to get it? How much of your real me has been lost in the process?

Identify which of your relationships are nourishing and which are toxic.

Toxic relationships are those that poison you with demands that you give up the real you in order to be a part of the relationship. Listen to the conversations you have with family and friends. How many times do you hear the respectful, "I'd really like your perspective on this," as opposed to, "You don't really *think* that, do you?" or, "You don't really *want* that," or "Don't feel that way"?

Nourishing relationships allow space and differences while toxic relationships demand constant availability and compliance. Nourishing relationships encourage independence, while toxic ones fester with unhealthy dependence. Nourishing relationships are inclusive and open, while toxic ones tend to be exclusive and closed. Nourishing relationships are enhanced by personal growth and change, while toxic ones are threatened by it. Nourishing relationships give room for alone time, while toxic ones intrude. Nourishing relationships respect the real you. Toxic ones require you to abandon your authenticity.

The Time Is Now

What changes in your thinking will allow you to make changes in your schedule? Do you see that you are valuable enough to be worth investing in, and that you need reflective time for growth? I don't know about you, but no one came along and told me to take the morning off, gave me permission to rest, or encouraged me to find a more creative way to manage my roles and responsibilities. That was a gift I had to give myself. When was the last time you gave yourself such a wonderful present?

How about giving yourself this gift now?

Personal Reflection

1. Finish this statement: I know I have a firm conviction that finding my true self is one of the most valuable things I can do because ...
2. Make a list of how you usually spend your time—not a detailed, minute to minute record, but a summary of your usual routine.

3. What roles do you fill? Make a list in your journal.

4. Name those who have a legitimate claim to your time. How much time do they legitimately need? Write a definition of a healthy, whole, nourishing relationship.

5. How do you attend to your own needs? Read Matthew 11:28 and also Isaiah 40:27-31. Taking time before the loving, living Father, what does He promise?

Prayerful Response

Dear Father, I'm thankful that You had people like me in mind when You said, "Come to me, all you who are weary and burdened, and I will give you rest. Take my yoke upon you and learn from me, for I am gentle and humble in heart, and you will find rest for your souls. For my yoke is easy and my burden is light" (Mt 11:28-30). I am weary, I am burdened and in need of rest. I want to take Your yoke. I want to learn. Show me, dear Lord. Amen.

SIX

You Are a "Work of Heart"

Have you ever looked around your house or apartment and wished you could get rid of all your belongings and start over?

I have. And though I was dead serious, I knew it was totally impractical—not to mention financially impossible. I knew it wasn't the furniture that caused my distress. It was my *life*.

Every one of us comes to passages in our lives where we *know* something has to change. We can't go on as we are any longer. Whatever the force that drives you, it will eventually lead to the same moment of truth: Life doesn't change to meet our needs; we are the ones who need to make the effort to change.

I have learned how to cooperate with God in working toward the changes that are needed within me—changes that make it possible for me to meet the demands of my life. Those

YOU ARE A "WORK OF HEART"   77

changes only come as I work for them, taking long looks at myself, understanding myself more and resisting the temptation to give in when I should press on. The changes come quietly, little by little, but nonetheless they are powerful and important—like the laying of new foundation stones on which the real me can stand at last.

You can expect the same sense of newfound strength and sturdiness in your life as the work of solitude allows the real you to emerge and grow.

As You Focus on God, God Works in You

When we stand before a great painting, or listen to the composition of a musical genius, we often refer to it as a "work of art." But what do we mean by that? Do we mean that the creator of such pieces worked at the art? Yes, in a way we do. But most of us are unaware of the inner dynamic that's at work in the true artist. Yes, the artist works hard for years at mundane tasks that help perfect his basic techniques, and teach him the basics of his chosen medium. But all the unexciting months of practice build a discipline that allow something greater to happen: *Discipline allows the art to work within the artist.* Beauty emerges because the artist makes the effort that allows the grace of beauty to appear.

In much the same way, something happens in us when we work at building solitude into our lives. When we develop the habit of purposeful withdrawal, solitude happens within us.

Solitude begins to teach us that we no longer need to be so

attached to other people's opinions and demands ... or even the comforts that company gives us. Solitude not only develops in us an independent mind and voice, it also hones our ability to distinguish God's voice amid the roar of voices demanding our allegiance. For, in the end, the power and grace that fill us in solitude come from God Himself.

Before we go any further, let me make this one point perfectly clear. Many advocate solitude for its healthy, and even "spiritual," benefits. But I'm not talking about merely making life better, or developing a personally designed monastic lifestyle aimed at making yourself a better person. I advocate the practice of periodic solitude as a spiritual discipline that makes you conscious of being in God's presence. In His presence alone can we learn more about who He has designed us to be, and what we are to do with our lives.

In Ephesians, Paul writes: "[God] is able to do immeasurably more than all we ask or imagine, *according to his power that is at work within us* ..." (3:20; italics mine). And in Philippians, Paul says we can be confident "that *he who began a good work in you will carry it on to completion* until the day of Christ Jesus" (1:6; italics mine). I urge you to embrace the discipline of solitude for these reasons: to allow God's power to work *within you* so that the good work of His power will *flow out of you*.

When we open ourselves fully to God, He begins a deep, life-changing, beautiful work in us—a true "work of heart."

It is my purpose to entice you to simply withdraw from the hurry and rush of the roles you fill. To release yourself from the rules by which you normally operate your life *so that the power and grace of God can change and mold you, working in your heart to give you perspective, strength, and wisdom.*

The Bible promises us that, if we open our hearts totally to God, we will know Him and know the path He has set for us. I have often encouraged myself with these truths, meditating on the beautiful words of Psalm 119:10-20 (emphasis mine), taking time alone to ponder them within my soul:

> *I seek you with all my heart;*
>   do not let me stray from your commands.
> *I have hidden your word in my heart*
>   that I might not sin against you.
> Praise be to you, O Lord;
>   *teach me your decrees.*
> *With my lips I recount* all the laws that come from your mouth.
> I rejoice in following your statutes as one rejoices in great riches.
> *I meditate on your precepts*
>   and *consider your ways.*
> *I delight in your decrees;*
>   I will not neglect your word.
> Do good to your servant, and I will live; I will obey your word.
> *Open my eyes* that I may see wonderful things in your law.
> *I am a stranger on earth;* do not hide your commands from me.
> *My soul is consumed with longing for your laws* at all times.

I have purposely marked with italics all the phrases that can only happen or be accomplished when I am alone. I'd like to suggest that you use this scripture as a meditational guide. Let's take a closer look, and I will show you what I mean.

With *All* My Heart

You may want to read through this section once, picking up on the personal responses I have recorded here. Then go back and record in your journal whatever thoughts, emotions, or responses are spurred by this Scripture:

I seek you with all my heart. Solitude gives me time to distance myself from those things that would fragment my heart and wear my emotions threadbare.

I have hidden your word in my heart. Tucked safely away in the corners of my heart are the healing promises of God's Word that supersede even my most painful childhood memories, the pain of violation and personal invalidation. The hope of God's Word can cover disappointment, restore vision, and bring back my joy.

Teach me your decrees. I no longer have to be defensive, or possessively hang on to my own interpretation of things in futile efforts at self-preservation. I can allow my heart to soften without fear of being destroyed. I can open my mind and consider other ideas or approaches to my problems. In other words, in solitude I find the safety needed to be teachable and trainable.

With my lips I recount. In solitude I can whisper my love for God. I can give in to my intense desire to praise Him with words not usually heard in the pat, acceptable phrases of my Bible study or prayer group. I can verbally express my most intimate feelings for God—there in His presence, within His hearing—alone.

I meditate on your precepts. No one can plumb the depth of God's ways or completely exhaust the "whys" of His will. But in solitude I can mull over the precepts of His Word until I understand them in the context of His will for me. Alone I can let His love reach out to me from the pages of His living Word.

Consider your ways. In solitude I can back off from good ideas and great plans for how I think my life should be run. I can allow the reality of a living and personal relationship with Jesus Christ to form His purposes within my heart and impact my mind.

I delight in your decrees. I can allow myself to feel, to take absolute delight in, God's ways and His plans, and His love for me. I can bathe myself in His justice, and know His ways are right for me.

Open my eyes. My vision is so limited. Solitude gives me time to think God-thoughts, to see God-things.

I am a stranger on earth. In solitude I recapture my status as an alien on earth, remembering I am a citizen of heaven. I remember that I am not at home in this world, I'm on a mission. No matter what I see going on around me, or happening to me—and no matter what I feel as a result of what's been done to me—*someday I'm going home.* When I spend time alone in God's presence, I remember that I'm not always going to be at ease here because the Fall of Man was never God's plan in the first place.

But while I'm here, my work is to know and become like Christ, then to glorify God by bringing a lost and dying world the news and hope of the risen and living Savior. My mission is to tell others not to get too comfortable here, because there is more, much more, for those of us who place our faith in God's Son.

My soul is consumed with longing for your laws. In solitude I can unplug from the world's system of determining what and who is important and worthy. I can step away from a humanistic, self-oriented society and experience firsthand what it's like to live guided by higher laws, to love at higher, purer standards. I can let my soul be consumed with something that will bring life and health to my whole person.

What you have just walked through is what I mean by "the work of solitude." But instead of a work of art, the Designer works within each of us His original work of *heart.* His heart. His love and His best intentions for our lives and families.

Can't you hear the heart of the Lover of our souls in the words of this magnificent passage:

My lover spoke and said to me, "Arise, my darling, my beautiful one, and come with me. See!

The winter is past; the rains are over and gone. Flowers appear on the earth; the season of singing has come, the cooing of doves is heard in our land. The fig tree forms its early fruit; the blossoming vines spread their fragrance. Arise, come, my darling; my beautiful one, come with me."

SONG OF SONGS 2:10-13

In Reply

What will be your response to the many invitations from Scripture to walk with God and to know Him? "Sorry, my precious Lord, but I have to stick another load of towels in the washer and take the dog to the groomer today"?

Or maybe your turndown will sound more spiritual than that. Maybe your refusal will come out of a sense of duty to serve others—and to do so in Jesus' name. Like so many, you may be too busy *doing for* Him to *be with* Him.

You and I can't be faulted for this emphasis on *doing* to the exclusion of *being*. We're far more likely to hear sermons that push us to take on more duty-bound, other-centered activities than we are to hear about solitude and taking time to be alone with God. Yet it doesn't matter that our culture—and even much of the church—lives and dies in a manic state. It is my responsibility—and it is yours—to reply to God's call, *"Come away!"* by making space in our lives to be alone with God, allowing Him to work in our hearts.

I must admit, for many years I ran from solitude. Now the thought of *not* incorporating alone time into my daily life is nearly unthinkable. Slowly, I am growing into the person that God intended me to be. Exposed to His gentle mercy, tender healing, and gentle encouragement, I am beginning to experience for myself the full meaning of Paul's statement: *"For we are God's workmanship ..."* (Eph 2:10). We are not just created by His hand, but are ongoing works of God's heart.

Personal Reflection

Record in your journal your responses to the following:

1. What struggles are you experiencing in your regular life because of taking time for solitude?

2. What inner struggle points surface because of taking alone time?

3. What is the "work of heart" that you'd like God to do in you?

4. What is there about God that has been denied or destroyed within you that you'd like restored to its rightful place or form?

5. I know I am God's own workmanship because ...

Prayerful Response

Dear Father, I often see myself as much less than a divine creation. Show me what You see in me, whisper to me of Your plans. Let me have something to grab on to for my security as I make these difficult and sometimes uncertain changes and let me rest secure in You. Amen.

SEVEN

Changing the Real Me

Reshaping my inner self means paying attention to myself. *This is hard.*

All my life, it seems I've been trained to do the exact opposite. In fact, when I think about it, the only times I've actually paid attention to myself are when I've determined something's *wrong with me* and I need *improvement*. We know the routine: lose a few pounds, get a makeover, take another class to upgrade or enhance our marketable skills, join another Bible study. None of these things are bad, but most attempts to make us better have little to do with relearning to be an authentic person. In fact, they may have more to do with becoming the *more presentable* you.

I often speak about "relearning" who we are, because so much of the *me* I present is learned. Along with good manners, other ideas programmed into me from the very beginning were: Don't rock the boat, don't fight back, watch your mouth, check your attitude, learn to get along, never ask for anything. These were all attempts to manage, if not force, me into being a "more acceptable, better approved" *me*.

Have you experienced the same?

Good behaviors and even furthering our education or taking another course can and often do help us get along in life, in church, at work, and in the family. Yet when all we care about is outward behavior, our true selves can begin to die, starved for attention, starved for the nurture we all need to become ourselves.

Why is it that we focus more on the outward person than on the real inner being? Marsha Sinetar explains it beautifully:

Some people learn to be compliant early in their lives. If their parents caution them against being seen or heard, against being uniquely themselves, if such lessons are learned too painfully, it is common sense that, as one option, they easily shut down their self-defining mechanisms and try to blend in with everyone else. Intimidated into conforming, they are punished into a safe, invisible way of being that can last a lifetime.[1]

Do I Dare to be Different?

Different. What a scary word. What if I become the real me and the people I hang out with, live with, and work with end up liking the old me—the one I presented so well—better? It's true, once the real you emerges, you may find your life changing, and even small changes can be frightening.

On the other hand, change can be good. When inner change means growing toward the person God designed you to be, it's always good. For me, this continues to be the most daring and courageous undertaking of my entire life.

This idea of personal growth might seem easier if we could go to some consultant or counselor and get a blueprint of what the real me is supposed to be—how we're supposed to proceed, and what it will cost. It would be so much easier. But I'm an original ... and so are you. There may be others who are a bit like you, but you're the only *you* God made. You're a designer's original, and no mass-produced pattern quite fits you. Again Marsha Sinetar offers insight:

> The socially transcendent individual has no ready-made routine, no like-minded others with whom to associate. Because there is no concrete blueprint for organizing a secular life dedicated to becoming more unique (which involves having more time to think, reflect, study, and commune with Self), each must necessarily design his own structure.[2]

Those of us who have accepted Christ and submit ourselves to God for our very lives know that becoming authentic must involve His work at the core of our efforts. It is in Him that we find our real selves, not only *created* but also *reflected*. There is no one like our God anywhere. Is it any wonder each of us was designed to be different? That's why changing and growing in Him mean: a new and exciting life—better than we had even just yesterday.

This growth and change also means something more. *We must be willing to be different from others.* If you were raised as I was, in a very legalistic environment, full of rules and proper ways to keep those rules, being different has always carried certain risks. In many cases, being an individual, unique, and original child was not only discouraged, it was *forbidden*.

But you and I are no longer children. Even if we were denied the opportunity to be our original selves as kids, what our parents or educators withheld from us we must withhold from ourselves no longer. The real me can be wonderfully excavated. We're not fossilized. We haven't been lost at sea. We are right here—and God's original blueprint still lies within each of us, awaiting rediscovery through nurturing and attention. *As adults, we owe it to ourselves and we owe it to God to let Him finish His original design.*

Proceed ... With Caution

It's only fair to warn you: Change isn't always comfortable. In fact, on many days, staying the same *presentable* people we've always been is a lot easier. It's like this: Once we manage to make any profound change in the way we handle life, especially as it relates to others, we can expect to feel a sense of emptiness and confusion—at least for a time. This is when we must be patient and prepared for emotional upheaval.

I began to experience this upheaval some years ago, when I made a simple change. As a young wife and mother, I decided the neighborhood coffee klatch wasn't for me. Neither was talking on the phone for hours with other young married women who were "stuck" at home with babies and house-work. At the time, I attended a very small and close-knit church, but unfortunately there was a lot of dysfunction among the membership. Everyone knew everything about everyone else. To maintain any privacy was perceived as being secretive and possibly even sinful. After all, if everything was out in the open, how could one harbor a secret sin? However, it wasn't a secret sin I was protecting—it was *me*. I needed time to think my own thoughts and form my own ideas and opinions. Spending hours and hours in coffee circles, or on shopping excursions, or on the phone drained me of my identity. I'd tried it, and could actually feel my individual personality slipping away. The more I engaged in being the presentable, acceptable person, the less I was able to maintain any sense of being myself.

I wanted out. Unable to find a way to cut back, or even momentarily withdraw, one day I just quit. I didn't answer the phone. I found excuses to stay away from coffee circles and even social events involving those who were sucking the life out of me emotionally and spiritually. Within a very short time I discovered that either you had to be all the way in or you were all the way out.

I felt abandoned and lonely. I had to look for ways to fill the hours formerly stolen from me on the phone and in coffee circles. It was months before I figured it out: I didn't belong to the group anymore because by nurturing my inner self, I no longer fit.

I didn't know what to call it at the time, but looking back I now understand that I was *transcending* some emotionally difficult, and spiritually destructive, ways that were being used to maintain so-called friendships. To stay healthy and true to myself, I was having to go it alone. That's when the battle of the will began: I wrestled with the question, "To fit in, or not to fit in?"

It was months before I could even begin to see that I had chosen a better way and that my willingness to undergo discomfort would actually lead to being more comfortable with who I was and where I would be heading in years ahead. I genuinely believe that if I had not decided to end such restrictive relationships, and if I hadn't had the courage to face whatever loneliness that would mean, I would never have taught my first Bible study, let alone written my first book. You see, those kinds of things were just not done in the former group. After all, we were all equals, and for someone to grow beyond the group threatened everyone. Growth and self-expression, and even ministry beyond our small circle, was discouraged, even sabotaged, by the others.

Looking back, I can now see that I was learning an important lesson. When you've lived as if the rules you obey and roles you fill make you authentic, then making even minor changes makes you feel like you're checking out on your own life. The truth is that when you make changes, you are giving up only what others have given—or, rather, what they have put on you. You are not giving up the real you. You are, in fact, giving birth to it.

Pick Your Battles Carefully

Change doesn't happen overnight. We need time to adjust, to formulate our own thoughts and ideas. We need space to let our true self grow roots and become healthy and secure. Because we need both time and space, it's wise to pick our personal battles carefully. Unless we're really comfortable with the changes going on inside, it's easy to slip back into old habits. For example, when I think becoming my real me is threatening or upsetting to another person, it's very easy to slip back into being the old, predictable me. Old patterns of being too dependable, too compliant, and too acceptable lie just within reach, even when I know they are not part of the real me.

How do we give ourselves encouragement and room to grow the secure roots we need? We take the pressure off by picking our battles carefully. I do this by making a conscious effort to keep in mind which issues are worth taking a stand for, and which are better left unaddressed. It's been freeing for me to realize that I will not die if someone gets the wrong impression of me, I will not suffocate if misunderstood or misinterpreted, and my world will not come crashing down if I let someone else believe they're right, even if I'm fairly sure that they are not. After all, my inner self needs nourishment and peace. It needs protection until the inner real me is expressed as naturally as the old compliant me. If I have to walk away from a battle now and then, or even give one up … so what? The real me will win in the long run.

It comes down to this: We need strength to be whole. The strength we found in personality, ability, or talent before is being replaced by a strength that comes from being our authentic selves.

But why do I refer to "picking our battles" at all? It's because life can suddenly be full of skirmishes when we begin to change, especially when those most closely related to us do not. Some of the people we care about most may not be willing to take the risk, or may not find the courage or grow to the depth of character necessary to change within themselves. This is when it is of utmost importance that we be able to look beyond the foibles and foolishness of others who are not experiencing the same growth we are. It takes a great deal of patience and maturity to be able to give to others without becoming emotionally scattered or swept away by their instabilities, pressures, or manipulations.

Thus, the work of solitude—the work of God within you—will most definitely make a difference in how you relate to others. In becoming the person God wants you to be, you will be more able to make and keep quality friendships. New relationships will blossom, and respect between you and those close to you will grow and thrive. This will threaten others. (How solitude benefits our ability to serve others will be covered in a later chapter, where we'll see how becoming authentic prepares us for servanthood.)

Change, Change, and More Change

Even the small changes we make now prepare us for those major changes we often need to make. Once our true selves begin to emerge, we begin to think differently about ourselves.

We see with far more clarity the bigger picture of our lives. We think differently about larger issues such as our goals, ministry activities, and family responsibilities. We begin to have a much clearer understanding of what in our lives needs to change, how to make those changes, and what things need to remain as they are. As we gain new respect for our inner selves, we begin to honor more deeply the call of God on our lives. As we take personal responsibility for the healthy maintenance of our inner lives, we appreciate more what we have to offer to others.

What I am defining here is *personal stewardship*. As Marsha Sinetar says, when you take charge of your life, "it may not conform to what society or family may expect from the individual."[3] The Bible says nearly the same thing, when Paul tells us: "Do not conform any longer to the pattern of this world, but be transformed by the renewing of your mind" (Rom 12:2).

Transformation takes time, and choices. After all, we expect vacations from work, sabbatical leaves from ministry, even retreats for women and men in our churches. But how many of us actually allow ourselves time away for restoration so that we can better handle the pressures of our closest priorities, our families, husbands, and children? Do we allow ourselves to make courageous new choices?

Making Courageous Choices

If we ever rediscover our authentic selves, it will be because we have the courage to make self-nourishing choices. Some choices will cause us to actively, aggressively reverse what life, people, and circumstances have delayed or denied in us until now.

Perhaps we don't even see that we have any choices—but we do. Choice is God-given. Maybe we have been so afraid or unwilling to *make* choices that we have almost lost the ability.

Choice is a very interesting biblical principle. I often turn to the Old Testament book of Deuteronomy to refresh myself in the biblical principle of choice. All through the book, God tells the people of Israel that He's going to make certain choices for them: where and how they will worship, where they will live, when and how they will mourn and celebrate. Over and over again, He repeats how important it is that they obey what He chooses for them. They must have realized that God's choice was to be followed by their obedience. But then, there come these startling words:

> I have set before you life and death, blessings and curses. Now choose life, so that you and your children may live....
> DEUTERONOMY 30:19

Almost without warning, they are told to choose. That's where we are now. We're about to choose. To make decisions based on becoming the women of God we were designed to be. To take time alone, with just the Lord's presence and His Word to give us guidance and support. With no comfort or encouragement except what He provides. It will take courage. Do you have that courage?

Here are choices you may need to make—choices that can bring the new you back to life.

Choose to bring order to chaos.

When I look back through my life, it's like looking down a barren stretch of highway with various-sized pieces of the real me lying scattered like so much litter along the way. How can I be individual? I gave that up as a child, trying to fit into an elementary teacher's mold. How can I be independent? I left that behind when I was nineteen. How can I have an opinion of my own? I threw that out when I was twenty-two, because I thought a "good wife" should think, act, and even vote like her husband. How can I choose to be different? I gave that up to the easier way of conformity and legalism years ago. You get the picture. My real self lies scattered through my past like pieces of a crash test dummy that didn't survive the test.

It's little wonder that the real me was in chaos.

To reclaim the real me, to bring order and serenity to my soul, it became necessary to outgrow such immature choices—to gather the pieces of my personal authenticity, to give myself the chance and the encouragement to change.

Choose to bring order to your thoughts.

To have the courage to think an issue through, instead of going the easier route of compliance, means we must first *make the decision to think for ourselves*. Then we must make the decision to bring order to our own authentic thoughts, and form our own conclusions.

For instance, we may not like the behavior of the president, but we don't have to agree with the critical, crude talk show host either. If we become orderly thinking people, it means that we may disagree with the pastor, but we don't have to join with the group that's trying to force his resignation. Make no mistake, however: independent choice comes only from an independent mind and spirit, and unless we give ourselves time to think and pray about issues, we may be swept in—even against our better judgment.

Choose to set your mind on the beautiful work of God in all things.
Choosing to give myself some alone time actually lets me experience something Paul talked about in Philippians, even when things trouble or frighten me:

> Finally, brothers, whatever is true, whatever is noble, whatever is right, whatever is pure, whatever is lovely, whatever is admirable—if anything is excellent or praiseworthy—think about such things.
>
> PHILIPPIANS 4:8

When I choose to become the person God made me to be, I can see the beauty, the patterns of God's work throughout my life more clearly—even on the darkest of days. You see, when we give ourselves freedom and take the responsibility to choose, to decide for ourselves, we give ourselves the chance *to see life from an entirely different perspective*. We embrace life from our own unique, God-given viewpoints. This makes possible the next real step of growth.

Choose character over compromise.
When I become the real me, God can begin to address my

deepest, inner self, the very core of my character. Settling for less than the real me means I have accepted, even acquiesced to, a life of shallowness and personal compromise.

Many years ago, I made it a life goal to become a woman of principle. You see, I had been defining myself by many early disappointments and personally traumatic events. It's true that early events shape us, but I'd become static. Eventually I began to understand that I had to break out of my old stoicism and find a new posture of choice, growth, and change. I discovered then that a woman of principle *chooses* to change, to grow, to become—and does not compromise when it comes to inner growth.

Choose to become responsive, rather than reactive.

One of the most exciting aspects of becoming authentic is the wonderful, healthy opportunity to relate to others from who we *are*, instead of how we *feel*. Responding from the real me is far different than reacting. When we become our true selves, our *doing* comes from our *being*.

Lisa found herself snapping at family, friends, and coworkers whenever she felt threatened by a remark, or even an imagined criticism. As she spent time alone, God seemed to focus on this touchiness. Why was she that way? Eventually, Lisa realized she was very insecure in her self because she was unsure about what she liked and didn't like, and about what she believed on many issues. When someone made even the slightest negative remark, she felt so unsteady and embarrassed, she snapped back in self-defense. Gradually, as she developed a healthy, authentic self, she was able to let negative comments roll past without taking them personally ... or else she would offer her own, positive opinion, out of newly sorted thoughts and beliefs, and let the other remark go. She was responding out of her being.

Choose to be patient with yourself as you grow.
Perhaps one of the most basic truths we all must learn is to be patient with ourselves as we grow into our true selves. Choosing to give yourself time to change is crucial. This means giving yourself both *plenty of time*—months and years—and the daily *gift of time*—in moments, hours, and weekend retreats.

Choosing to give myself time to change means I have given myself a timeless treasure—the gift of individuality, wholeness, and authenticity. It's the same for you.

Personal Reflection

Take some time right now to consider these questions about choices that God can empower you to make:

1. If you were to choose to bring order to chaos, would that have more impact on your inner attitudes or actual practical considerations as you rethink earlier decisions?

2. When you think of bringing order to your thoughts, how would you go about doing that?

3. If you choose to set your mind on the beautiful work of God in all things, what things will you have to think about less? More?

4. What do the following mean to you?

Choosing character over compromise.

Choosing to become responsive, rather than reactive.

5. How can you choose to be more patient with yourself as you grow?

Prayerful Response

Dear Father, I realize that You have given me the freedom of choice, and with that freedom, responsibility for those choices. Show me where I've made irresponsible and unwise choices and help me make new ones if necessary. Give me the strength and courage to stand by the good choices I've made. Amen.

EIGHT

Honoring the Real Me

"**H**ow do you honor yourself?" I asked my friend Katie.

"Honor myself?" She looked blank. "I can't imagine doing that. In fact I give myself as little attention as possible. I spend as much time honoring others as I possibly can, but to honor myself seems totally self-centered and fleshly."

"Fleshly?" I inquired.

"Yeah. Because getting in touch with all my feelings, hopes, and dreams only dredges up disappointment. It's too painful to think about what I don't have that I *wanted* to have at this point in my life. So I just give all my attention to my family and my job."

"But you seem so fulfilled," I replied.

"Fulfilled? I really don't know. I'm so busy I never think about it."

"Where did you leave the real you?" I asked.

"I don't know and I don't care," said Katie. "In fact, it's more than not caring—I don't want to know."

How sad. Somewhere, perhaps years ago, my friend faced a crossroads. And instead of dealing with the disappointment in her life, she shrugged her shoulders and let her real life slip from her fingers.

I made that observation, and asked, "When did that happen?"

Katie grew thoughtful. "The first time was at baby number three, and the last time at baby number four." She sighed. "Both were unplanned. Don't get me wrong, I love my kids, and wouldn't take anything to give them up. But I sure didn't plan this."

So, can't a woman have a family and love even those unexpected, unplanned additions without giving up her authentic self? There must be a way to maintain loyalty both to oneself and to other responsibilities, such as family, work, and church. Sadly, Katie isn't the only one who has seen this as an either/or situation. Yet it doesn't have to be that way. With a few adjustments to your life and priorities, the real you can be honored along with your other commitments. It doesn't have to mean either taking care of them or taking care of me. Integrated, whole people manage responsibilities to both their true selves and the rest of their lives.

When people in our culture speak of honoring your true self, they're often referring to putting yourself first and everything and everyone else on hold. Then, if there's any time or energy left, you'll consider the needs of others. That is *not* what I'm talking about here. I'm not advocating an "I come first and the rest of you get in line" attitude.

On the other hand, Christian women often put everyone and everything else first, putting their authentic selves on hold. That's not a balanced approach to honoring the people God has created us to be.

Real Needs of the Real Me

Most women I know maintain two kinds of lists that rule their lives. The first list is "Their Needs"—those of husband, children, parents, and boss. The second list is "My Needs." Only when all of *their* needs are covered do we turn to our needs. But by then we're too tired, our resources are drained, and the list of *their* needs is already growing again. Then what? We begin all over again, seeing to *their* needs, neglecting and ignoring our own. Once again, the real me is shoved to the side or forgotten.

The answer is not to neglect others' needs, but to recognize the importance of tending to your own as well.

How can we be true to *their* needs and our authentic selves, too?

We begin by *honoring* our true selves, turning to God's Word for guidance. Return with me to Psalm 119. In chapter five we looked at certain verses, but now I want to take a different focus. At one point, the psalmist asks: *How can a young man keep his way pure?* For our purposes, this question might be put in the form of a prayer:

How can a woman make sure she is pure in her motives when being true to her real me?

How can we make sure that when we take this adventure inward we don't end up selfish and carnal in our attitudes toward others?

The answer is: *By living according to your word* (v. 9).

Our first step in honoring our real me is to live true to God's Word. Who does God say we are to put first? Once again the Bible has the answer: *I seek you with all my heart* (v. 10). God comes first. Not your family, not you, not God's other children—God Himself. Consider these Scriptures, as well:

Acknowledge the God of your father, and serve him with wholehearted devotion and with a willing mind, for the Lord searches every heart and understands every motive behind the thoughts. If you seek him, he will be found by you....

1 CHRONICLES 28:9

Seek first his kingdom and his righteousness....

MATTHEW 6:33

Second, as born-again children of the most Holy God, we honor ourselves only as we honor Him first. Then, we bring Him our needs, prayers, dreams, hopes. Yes, that's right. Honor God first, then honor your true self next. I know what many of you are thinking at this moment. The words and melody of the old familiar Sunday school chorus may be ring-

ing loudly in your memory: *Jesus, others, and you spells J-O-Y.*
But does it? Most of us have lived our lives with just the Jesus
and others part. That only spells *J-O*—far short of complete
joy. But when we put ourselves at the feet of the King as a part
of our regular routine, even separating ourselves from others,
we honor both Him and our true selves. Perhaps we could
reword the old song to say: *Jesus, ourselves, and* then *you, spells*
J-O-Y.

The Courage of Our Convictions

Third, honoring the real me means we will form convictions
based on our relationship with God and our knowledge of His
Word. That takes place as we honor Him first and our true
selves next. Marsha Sinetar says:

> People are whole when they have the guts to live out their
> convictions in their lives, when they can face difficult situa-
> tions and everyday choices in a way that honors what's inside
> them....[1]

Simply being in His presence, exposing the authentic me to
Him without reservation gives me that kind of courage. When
I'm secure in those convictions, I'm able to honor the real me
as I face the rest of life with its choices and challenges.

To honor the real me means to know for certain what we
stand for and what we're against. We know which causes to
take up and which to let go. Honoring the real me means I can

form a positive self-definition: I can learn to know and be confident in who I am and what I'm about and be hopeful about where I'm going from here. Honoring the real me means I can stand by my personal principles and preferences. I can live without compromise.

I would venture to guess that there are many Christian women who live in compromise without even knowing it because they've never taken the time to form their own base for convictions and personal principles. My friend Julia is definitely *not* one of those women.

Julia's husband has recently been enticed by suggestive, unsolicited e-mail advertising. In the privacy of his own home he dropped his guard, and within a few months he was not only visiting the X-rated web sites, but bringing some of the practices and behaviors back to Julia for experimentation. Julia had reservations, even though her husband was a Christian. "The marriage bed is undefiled," he said. She almost dropped her guard. After all, she was tempted to reason, he is the head of the house, the priest in the household. Isn't a Christian wife supposed to submit?

However, Julia had made it her habit to honor God first, and her authentic self next. Very quickly she knew that her husband had been snared. She knew that God's Word doesn't say the marriage bed is automatically undefiled. In fact, God's Word is very strong and perfectly clear when it says, "Marriage should be honored by all, and the marriage bed kept pure, for God will judge the adulterer and all the sexually immoral" (Heb 13:4).

Courageously standing by her convictions, she lovingly confronted her husband about his demands and suggested they disconnect the Internet server and see a counselor. Having strength that comes from honoring both God and her true self, she was ready to face the consequences of her choices. Fortunately, her husband was willing to face the truth of what he was doing and soon asked his wife for forgiveness and repented before God, as well.

Having the courage of her convictions and honoring her true self saved Julia from compromise and kept her husband from continuing down a spiritually destructive pathway.

Unfortunately, I know of another young woman who had to be willing to go it alone rather than compromise herself, even with her husband. Honoring God and her true self led her to examine God's Word, then to counselors, and finally to court— because her husband would not give up or get help for his addiction to pornography.

Am I saying that if a husband (or someone else) doesn't live up to God's Word, we should simply kick him out and go on with our lives? No, not at all. These two cases are examples of how two women lived by the courage of their convictions. They both judged behavior by the standard of God's Word. That ability and strength came out of being in close relationship with Him and being true to their authentic selves. Both had developed their own understanding of what was truly valued and what they personally held in high esteem. According to the standard of God's Word, purity within marriage was a priority. Compromise was out of the question.

In some ways, you could say they embraced a new discipline— they were willing to be responsible *for*, as well as *to*, their true selves.

Honoring yourself is more than just honoring God, being aware of and attentive to your own needs, and living without compromise. It is also learning to nurture the real you. It is to this subject that we now turn our attention.

Personal Reflection

Take some time to think before you answer the following questions:

1. Whose needs do you put before your own?

2. How do those needs rate before your own? For example, do your kids really need you to run their forgotten homework to school more than you need an occasional morning of uninterrupted quiet and rest? Does the ladies' auxiliary or women's ministry department in your church really need you to make the centerpieces more than you need less to do? Do you really have to hostess the meeting, make the dessert, *and* teach the Bible study? How do you rate the needs of others, compared to your own?

3. List some areas where standing by the convictions of your true self would mean you need to be strong in the face of pressure to neglect yourself.

4. What are some valid reasons for taking care of someone else's needs and ignoring or putting on hold your own?

5. List some needs of your own that you've been neglecting. How do you have to change your schedule or attitude to take more responsibility for those needs?

Prayerful Response

Dear heavenly Father, I see that I have been neglecting my own needs. Maybe I've been running away from them, even using the needs of others as an excuse to neglect the inner work of my own needs. Forgive me, Lord, for tending to those needs in others that only You can meet. Meet me at this vulnerable, open level and show me my own heart and help me tend to my own backyard before pulling weeds in someone else's. Amen.

NINE

Nurturing the Real Me

We're such good nurturers of others. We tend to others' needs, often to the neglect of our own. In fact, if we're brutally honest, many of us will admit we've been taught to do so. We're good at appearing to be emotionally independent, even when we are quite the opposite. I don't know about you, but it's not that unusual for me to want and need emotional support, then when I don't get it, blame myself for needing it.

As I've learned to honor the real me, I've had to train myself to speak up, to let those closest to me know I have certain needs, and what they can do to help me. Just as importantly, I've learned when to take responsibility for meeting my own emotional needs in ways that do not ask those in my life for what they cannot give. In either case, honoring the real me means I have to learn to be responsible for my own emotional needs. It's what we call *nurturing*.

Nurturing the Real Me

Although I love being alone, I'm also a "people person." I can make myself feel good just by being around other people. I can even indirectly nurture myself by nurturing someone else. Yet there are times when I need to take responsibility for nurturing myself *directly*. I have not found this easy. I have to do on purpose what others may do naturally. Let the following list help you understand more about nurturing the real you.

First, nurturing the real me means periodically identifying emotional needs that are not met.
For example, in a quiet time before God you might notice that you've been lonely a lot lately, so you make a note in your journal that you need more social contact.

Personally, it's easy for me to neglect my social needs because I am very comfortable being by myself. If I'm not careful to maintain balance, I can soon feel lonely without being able to put my finger on the cause. Sometimes I sense anger or unforgiveness creeping in, making me critical, or giving me a jaundiced view of life in general. Then I use the pattern of Psalm 51, asking God to examine me for unconfessed sin or sinful attitudes.

You see, identifying our emotional needs helps us honor God by applying His Word to those emotions. We honor our true selves when we give those emotions the attention they deserve. Sometimes our emotional needs aren't so spiritual. We may need more romance or softness in our lives. Occasionally, we may notice that we've let the quality of our emotional life slip and become stagnant. We may notice cobwebs in the soul. This leads to the second item on our nurture list.

Second, nurturing the real me means doing something or giving myself something wonderful toward meeting those needs.

For me, this is usually not that hard. It might be a moment alone, a cup of cappucino, lunch with a friend, a long-distance phone call without watching the time, or reading a whole novel in one day. Sometimes it's as simple as lighting candles on my table at suppertime, listening to soft music, or using my loveli-est china teacup. Maybe it's taking up a handicraft or making biscotti on a rainy afternoon. Anything that helps and supports me emotionally will fill the bill.

Third, nurturing the real me means learning not to take responsibilities that are not mine to begin with.

Nurturing the real me means I need to learn to establish healthy emotional boundaries.

You will soon learn that honoring the real me does not per-mit us to take on anyone else's responsibilities—after all, don't we each have enough responsibilities of our own? The Bible makes it clear that we are to help carry each other's burdens (see Gal 6:2), but that's quite different from assuming an-other's responsibilities. The apostle Paul goes on to say that each of us should carry our own load (see Gal 6:5).

Begin to establish healthy boundaries—that is, know where you end and others begin. Understand and honor the tasks and burdens that truly belong to you and learn how to encourage others as they balance their own loads. Every person in your world has a true self that needs to grow. When you take on others' responsibilities, you dishonor not only your true self, but theirs as well.[1]

Fourth, nurturing the real me does sometimes mean doing something for someone else.

It's especially enriching to me to make someone a handmade gift or greeting card. For others it may be self-nurturing to make a pot of soup or stew for a sick neighbor or friend. It's not that unusual to find boxes or bags of garden-grown vegetables on the countertop at our church office, as people nurture others with the product of their work in the garden.

Fifth, we nurture our authentic selves by reestablishing personal priorities.

When we make wholeness a personal priority, we give a place of importance to honoring our inner being.

We make wholeness a priority by listening to inner intuitions. We make it a priority when we validate personal pain, and when we understand our limitations and weaknesses. And we nurture ourselves when we give ourselves permission and the encouragement needed to keep trying and growing in spite of our pain or limitations. To be whole will require us to give our true selves the opportunity and patience needed to grow until we are wholly restored.

Sixth, nurturing the real me can mean rewriting the rules by which we live.

This may be one of the hardest tasks we have to do. We've lived by unspoken rules for so long that we have a hard time sorting them all out. In addition to the rules of our Christian subculture, we also feel the pressure of rules placed upon us by the culture at large and by our families.

How do we know when the rules are crushing our true

selves? How do we go about rewriting those rules that are not God-honoring? Once again we turn to the rock-solid foundation of God's Word.

> Do not conform any longer to the pattern of this world, but be transformed by the renewing of your mind. Then you will be able to test and approve what God's will is—his good, pleasing and perfect will.
>
> ROMANS 12:2

Because we are interested in something far more valuable than "self improvement" ... because our goal is the reclaiming of our true selves ... what we need is *transformation*. By renewing our minds in God's Word, and by walking closely with Him in solitude, we come to look at life from an entirely different point of view. We begin to separate and detach from the will of the world, and we begin to make the will of God our standard. Released from the should's and shouldn'ts of our upbringing, we nurture our true selves by taking responsibility for being conformed to the Word of God. Then, renewed in our minds, we live transformed and changed lives.

Seventh, we nurture our true selves by reclaiming wants and hopes.
What have you hoped for? What have you wanted for your life? It's not too late. It's not too hard. It's not out of reach. Your dreams, as well as my own, are reasonable, hope-filled, and possible. Some of our problems stem from settling for too little, rather than reaching for too much.

The Bible says,

Since, then, you have been raised with Christ, set your hearts on things above, where Christ is seated at the right hand of God. Set your minds on things above, not on earthly things.

COLOSSIANS 3:1-2

How many women have settled for the earthly offerings of materialism, position, or a career? We are more than our belongings or social standing or what we do. We are children of the Most High God.

Are you concerned that your wants and hopes are not of God? Then follow the advice of the psalmist, who tells us:

Delight yourself in the Lord and he will give you the desires of your heart.

PSALM 37:4

It's time we honored and nurtured our authentic selves by delighting ourselves in the Lord and letting Him give us the liberty of being filled with hopes and dreams. Go ahead, I dare you—*hope again.*

Eighth, we nurture our true selves by learning a responsive approach to life.

How easy it is to get into a reactive, rather than a responsive mode in coping with our daily lives and the situations that throw themselves against our best efforts to be whole and complete. It's one thing to involuntarily shift into an adrenaline rush when the phone jangles you awake in the middle of the night, but many of us live as if every unexpected circumstance is a potential emergency. Instead of living in "stress mode," take a deep, self-nurturing breath before taking on the challenges tossed your way each day.

God's Word reminds us:

Do not be anxious about anything, but in everything, by prayer and petition, with thanksgiving, present your requests to God. And the peace of God, which transcends all understanding, will guard your hearts and your minds in Christ Jesus.

PHILIPPIANS 4:6-7

Finally, we nurture ourselves by releasing the real me to be real.

Nothing dishonors the real me like perfectionism. Unreal expectations, demands that we meet every struggle with strength and every tragedy with triumph—these are sure setups for slipping back into roles and rules that are not part of our authentic selves. Sorrow is heavy and failure is painful. Sometimes the burdens of life are too heavy to be carried alone, and we need to be able to admit when our true selves are weary.

I love these tender words of help and grace from the Bible:

Therefore, since we have a great high priest who has gone through the heavens, Jesus the Son of God, let us hold firmly to the faith we profess. For we do not have a high priest who is unable to sympathize with our weaknesses, but we have one who has been tempted in every way, just as we are—yet was without sin. Let us then approach the throne of grace with confidence, so that we may receive mercy and find grace to help us in our time of need.

HEBREWS 4:14-16

What I am saying, in plain English, is *cut yourself some slack.* Give yourself a break!

This is *not* the same as giving yourself permission to sin or be faithless. Nor am I encouraging you to drop your guard, stop praying, or be unprepared. I'm saying, *be real.* Sometimes life is hard, even for healthy, whole, fully nurtured people.

It's Up to You—Really

The message within these last two chapters—about the nurture of ourselves—can seem strange and selfish indeed for those of us who have been conditioned to feel that our inner needs are not a high priority or that nurturing the self is "sinful." Perhaps you've never given any thought to making wholeness your priority by honoring and nurturing your true self. But let me ask you this: *If you don't take this responsibility, who will?*

While you think about what I've presented, why not refer to the passages in God's Word and review these concepts as they apply to your own life. This would be a good time to write your responses in your journal.

Personal Reflection

1. Which of the self-nurturing suggestions I've listed in this chapter do you already do? List some of the ways in which you can improve the way you nurture your true self.

2. How painful is it to identify emotional needs that are not met? How can prayer help you manage that pain?

3. How hard is it *not* to take responsibilities that are not yours to begin with? Be specific and write out an example of responsibility you've taken on that you'd like to release. What would you have to do, or not do, for that to happen? What would be the consequences of making this change?

4. When was the last time you did something or gave yourself something wonderful, just because...? What could you do or give yourself now?

5. Are you more reactive or responsive in your approach to life? Which approach helps you live true and honoring to yourself? How does your approach help or hinder you in releasing your real me?

Prayerful Response

Help me, Lord, to know the difference between what You've given me to do and what others would like me to do. Show me the areas where I overstep my own healthy boundaries and neglect my own needs in the process. Teach me which personal responsibilities I neglect and how to shoulder my own normal load and encourage the others in my life when I see them trying to do the same. Amen.

TEN

Honoring Your Real Needs

Previously, we saw that one way we honor our true selves is to acknowledge our inner needs. As women, we do have certain emotional needs, that's true. But we have other deep needs as well.

It's not easy—in fact it can be quite difficult—for many of us to be truthful about our needs. Betsy is ashamed of the need she has to lead, remembering all her early training that women are to remain in the background. Janice denies her need for beauty and culture, something in which her husband and sons have no interest. Martina browbeats herself for wanting a week away from everything, when her aging mother needs constant care.

Even women of keen insight and unwavering personal conviction can find it takes enormous courage and strength to admit their real needs. Personally, I know how important it is to be truthful about my inner needs. Even so, I can still feel the inner opposition, and have to work against a tendency to ignore or neglect those needs.

Working Against Ourselves

The truth is, *personal honesty and self-revelation is always risky*. Even admitting our needs to ourselves often flies in the face of everything we've been taught. But there is something more frightening to face: Acknowledging inner needs forces us to confront our values—and that means we may have to adjust or abandon what we once perceived to be biblical truth. In short, *once we acknowledge our inner needs, we may be required to grow*.

Furthermore, it's not that easy to give credence to what we want, what we are, and the inner needs of our true self. To pay attention to the needs of the authentic self—to honor and nurture oneself at this level—can be misunderstood by others as being selfishly introspective. Another huge risk. Just the thought of being judged as self-centered keeps many women from even knowing their true selves, let alone honoring their inner needs.

"I don't know," a young professional woman told me recently. "I want to get a raise. And in order to get it, I need to sign up for those continuing education courses. But I'm not sure I should spend that kind of money on myself."

"I know what you mean," said another. "I can't really justify getting myself a computer so I can work at home. So we're going to buy one for the kids for Christmas."

"Will they get to use it?" I asked.

"Maybe," she laughed. "I just can't bring myself to admit we're spending all that money on me."

Using the kids as an excuse can come in handy when we live with self-doubts about how much our true needs deserve. The desire to please others can be nearly impossible to overcome. We've all heard the stories of the sacrificial mother who cut up her good coat to make smaller ones for her children. Or the one who passed over the new Sunday dress, preferring to buy Easter bonnets for her daughters. Many women my age were raised by mothers who lived through the Great Depression era, and although our material and financial situations are nothing like those impossibly difficult days, guilt motivates us to push aside our true needs as if they were.

Unless we make a brave attempt to address our real needs, we'll be stuck right here, with a presentable me, but with a frustrated longing for the real me to grow and thrive. We may spend our whole lives hungering for the life God created us to have—but convinced we're not worth the effort. Unless we're willing to drop the facades of self-protection and learn to nourish the innermost self, we jeopardize our chances of living our lives to the fullest. We continue to work against ourselves.

Facing the Challenge

Producing the real me is a huge personal challenge. We know it instinctively.

"I feel terrible," one woman said. "If I set aside time to take care of my own needs then find someone else's needs have been overlooked. I'm overwhelmed with guilt."

"I went on retreat once," said another. "I really needed a break. But I came back to a house full of dirty dishes, and fast food containers everywhere. The hot water heater had sprung a leak and flooded the entire basement. My husband was furious and the kids were upset. Suddenly, I felt as if all the mishaps of their entire Saturday were my fault—that if I'd been home taking care of their needs instead of my own, none of this would have happened."

Many of us know that feeling, don't we? We also know that hot water heaters don't actually wait to leak until we leave the house. It just seems like it. The garbage disposal isn't just listening until we leave so it can jam. But judging by the enormous load of guilt we shoulder when things go wrong in our absence, we obviously believe at some deep level that the responsibility for everyone's total well-being rests on our shoulders.

"I set aside my needs in a totally different way," says my friend Nadine. "I kept putting them off until I could lose some weight. I refused to shop for a new dress, or get a perm. I even refused to go on a cruise for my twenty-fifth anniversary, because I thought I should be thin first. I passed up an opportunity to teach Sunday school because I thought I wasn't a good example. All because I wanted to lose a few pounds first and make myself presentable to other people."

I know what Nadine feels and thinks about herself. Once I, too, put off living until I could lose weight. In my case, forty or fifty pounds. Many women neglect their true selves because their sense of body image tells them they are not "worth" the attention right now. In the back of their minds they tell themselves, *If the outer me will just shape up, then maybe the real me will be worth the attention.* Sad, but too many of us live by this wrong and crippling belief.

How do we face the challenge of meeting real needs? Although this can be difficult, and requires a bit of courageous effort, it's not as hard as we think. To honor your real needs means that you must start treating yourself as a real person, with valid thoughts, concerns, dreams, and desires. As you will find, these needs are far deeper than our emotions—they spring out of our core beliefs and values.

Needs of the Real You

One of the greatest needs of the real me is the need to believe in ourselves—especially in our true selves. We need to believe in ourselves, not because we've achieved some magnificent accomplishments, but because we are women made in the image of God, with God-given interests and loves.

Because God believes in you, *choose to believe in yourself.*

It's on this basis that we can accept our hopes and dreams as having worth and value. In light of the fact that the values in our heart have been shaped by God, we stop listening to those voices, within and without, that say, *You must be crazy ... or selfish.*

Do you dream of designing your own clothes, or writing a story? Your dreams have worth. Do you want to build a business, or climb mountains? Value your aspirations. Your real me needs you to value your hopes and dreams. Have you longed to learn to play a musical instrument or change the oil in your car? If it's your dream, it's important. Whether or not anyone else believes in your true self, God does.

Another need of the authentic self is the need to be *celebrated*.

Now, it's hard to celebrate being you when you are always wishing you were someone else. Stop coveting someone else's life and start celebrating your own. Stop living in someone else's shadow and start casting one of your own.

You may protest that there's nothing much to celebrate. If so, it's time you took a look at some of your other real needs.

Your true self needs you to acknowledge your gifts.
Your gifts are those things you do with ease, as if you were born with the ability. Usually we think of talent as belonging to those we define as "gifted."

For example, I don't know how I do it, but I can put furniture in a room, hang a few pictures, toss a few pillows here and there, and it looks like I hired a decorator. Some of my friends struggle with furniture placement and fabric swatches, plan down to the smallest detail, and still, in frustration, call me in to help. I simply move a plant or angle a chair or table and it comes together perfectly. I have what's called "the touch." It's a gift.

My friend Joy, on the other hand, is gifted differently. Her house always looks like she has just cleaned it. Mine never does. I observed her for several years when our kids were little. I struggled; she didn't. I spent enormous effort trying to keep my house clean and tidy; she never did. I read books on organization and time management; not her. She was born with the ability to keep her house with apparently little effort. It's her gift.

I have another friend who plays the piano and sings beautifully. After only a few lessons, by junior high she was playing for church services and singing solos. What most of us could never accomplish she does with ease. It's her gift.

A precious lady at my church seems to always be in the right place at the right time with just the right tool or resource in her hand. She knows when a file cabinet needs attention. She knows how to run the copy machine, and is on hand to fold the bulletin each week. No one has to tell her what needs to be done—she just knows naturally. It's her gift.

A woman who lives in the next town grows her own roses, dries them, and, using a variety of locally grown moss and evergreens, forms them into exquisite floral arrangements, swags, and wreaths. She has such a special touch, you can recognize her work immediately. It's her gift.

My friend Laurel has a remarkable gift for coming up with event themes and knowing how to carry those themes out down to the smallest detail. Go to an event at her church and you will find the most unusual items carrying out her unique themes. Junk stores, thrift shops, and overstock discounters are her favorite haunts. It's her gift.

I stayed recently in the home of a woman who has accessorized her entire home with Salvation Army store treasures. She has an eye for what others may consider trash or junk. Her house could be featured in *Victoria* or *Better Homes and Gardens*. It's her gift.

Think about it: What do you do that comes naturally? Are you a good organizer or motivator? Do you cook or paint? Do you put children at ease, or do other women trust you with their secrets? Do you garden or sew? Are you more apt to chair a committee or offer support?

Can you plan activities or host dinner parties with ease? Is your flair table decorations or oil painting? Are you an artist at cross-stitch, or a happy meals-on-wheels volunteer? Every one of us has "giftings." To meet your own real me needs, you must acknowledge your gifts.

Know your passions.

What makes you cry? What makes you angry? What can make you toss all caution aside to act, volunteer, or give toward a cause? Honoring your real me needs requires that you pay attention to what moves you.

Beth makes quilts for the homeless. Barbara organizes neighborhood lunch or tea parties, loving her neighbors to Jesus. Sharon has a passion for animals and voluntarily heads the local animal adoption efforts. Pat works in a neonatal unit, lovingly, tirelessly, sacrificially spending her life and emotions giving high-risk newborns the best possible chance to survive. Sarah serves relentlessly alongside her youth-pastor husband because of her passion for teens. Grace fills her pantry with food for those in crisis or family emergency. Lori and Leslie put themselves and their reputations on the line to run a crisis pregnancy center. Mentoring moms in my church community involve themselves with pregnant teens who opt to deliver rather than abort their babies.

Something moves each of us. Deep within our true selves we each feel passionately about something. Your true self needs you to be attentive to your own passions. You need to recognize what causes, conditions, or ministry opportunities touch you at your deepest.

Know where you fit.
We all need to belong. Our gifts need expression, our passions an outlet. Knowing where you fit will enable you to give your real me needs a place to be satisfied. Look at your gifts, understand your passions, and then find a place to use them. Most likely, it will be exactly where you fit. Your real me needs to fit—to belong and to be honored.

Do you fit in an educational setting? Your passions will most likely tell you who to teach, and your gifts, what to teach.

My passion for Christ and love for His people, combined with my communication abilities, makes my writing and retreat ministry fit perfectly. My passion for solitude makes my study and research that much easier. The other side of my personality—the "people person" side—makes bringing the fruit of my solitary work to others a joy.

One of my closest friends has a passion for what some might consider "throw-away" children. Combine that with her love of home and family and her ability to make anyone feel welcome and you can guess that her life as a foster parent has been more than successful. She fits in well with schoolteachers, parents, and social workers. Despite her busy, demanding life, it's no wonder she's often sought out to teach classes on parenting skills. She fits her life and her life fits her.

Look for "Open Doors"

Once you know what your gifts are, recognize your passions, and know where you will fit, you can begin to look for open doors of opportunity. In the wonderful course *Experiencing God,* the authors challenge Christians to look for where God is working and join Him there. I would add, look for a place where God is already at work that fits with your gifts and passions and see if you don't fit perfectly in that ministry or activity. Needs are present on every side. One only has to look down the pew on any given Sunday to see people who need love and attention. In fact, it can be overwhelming and confusing. So many needs, so many hurting people. It's not finding a place to serve that's problematic, it's finding the most effective and efficient place to serve—a place that doesn't overlook our authentic needs but honors them by putting our gifts, passions, and need to belong to good and productive use. It isn't ministry we need, but *fruitful* ministry.

You see, I firmly believe that many of us operate out of a limited, discounted sense of our true selves. And I'm convinced that in doing so we not only limit what we are capable of, but we also adversely affect the very ministries or organizations we long to help. When we operate out of integrated, whole selves, however, we bring quality to whatever opportunities open to us. Instead of constantly searching for and seeking God's will, *God's will seems to find us.*

Is this too big a dream for you? Is this too much to hope for or ask? I want to remind you again of what Paul says:

[God] is able to do immeasurably more than all we ask or imagine, according to his power that is at work within us.

EPHESIANS 3:20

Let His power work within you. Let Him show Himself through the gifts He's placed within you. Pay attention to the passions He planted within your heart and look for the place where He wants to bring it all together for the good of His kingdom.

No Dream Too Big ... None Too Small

There is no dream too big, and, conversely, there is no task too small. Nothing God puts into your hands that brings together your gifts and passions while providing a place for you to be genuine and real as you work for His glory can be defined as insignificant or small. Whether it's changing diapers or changing lives, if it's writing encouraging notes or life-changing books, if it presents an opportunity for your gifts and passions to be used by God, your true self touches eternity.

Isn't it time you attended to the needs of your true self? I think so.

Personal Reflection

1. Look up Psalm 37:4. In light of that verse, how can you accept your hopes and dreams as having worth and value?

2. Second Corinthians 10:12-13 says: "We do not dare to classify or compare ourselves with some who commend themselves. When they measure themselves by themselves and compare themselves with themselves, they are not wise. We, however, will not boast beyond proper limits, but will confine our boasting to the field God has assigned to us." Think of your abilities as "the field" to which God has assigned you. What gifts or talents did He give you? How have you encouraged them? How have you neglected them?

3. What touches your deepest emotions? Is there a cause or situation that affects you so that you toss all caution aside to act, volunteer, or give? Make a list of what you feel passionate about.

4. Seeing your gifts, knowing your passions, name several places or ministries where you might fit. How do you use your time now? Do your activities and employment honor your true self? If not, what would it take to make a change?

5. Think of one place you might serve that wouldn't overlook your authentic needs but, in fact, would honor them by putting your gifts, passions, and need to belong to good and productive use. What would it take to get involved there? What would you have to give up? What would you have to learn? Who would you have to contact to get started? Why would you hesitate? Read Ephesians 2:10. How can that verse become a reality for you?

Prayerful Response

There are times, my Father, when I want to abandon _____ (name that which you feel isn't your real ministry or place of belonging) and instead honor the true self you created in me by getting involved in _____ (name that which seems to draw you, heart and all). Dear Lord, help me to see where I belong and what You've designed me to be. Let my days and heart-driven efforts become fruitful ministry in Your kingdom. In Jesus' name, amen.

ELEVEN

Honoring
Your Body

The real you lives within your body. I know that seems like a strange, almost needless comment, but if you're like me, an American female, your authentic self can be denied and even lost in our culture's obsession with physical perfection.

In my book *Loved On a Grander Scale* I wrote about my diet history and how interwoven it had become to my Christian testimony. It began with an offhand comment about my fourteen-year-old body and persisted until I was forty-five. Thirty-one years of preoccupation with my size had tangled itself around my sense of worth, strangling what I perceived to be my usefulness in God's kingdom. When size or appearance is of such importance, it's not surprising that for many women, changing an unsightly feature or shedding unwanted pounds becomes a lifetime goal.

Do You Love Your Body?

For me, body image was an emotional land mine, and the repercussions were felt at their full impact for most of my adolescent and adult life. That one fateful day at fourteen, everything I thought about myself changed. Life took on a dark overtone: I was unlovely, unacceptable, and undesirable, or so I thought, simply because I was large. From that moment forward I had one pressing responsibility—one mission in life—to become thin. It became my challenge, and I took my weight on as if it were the most important issue in my entire life. I even began to believe that any struggle, any rejection or relational difficulty I encountered, was a result of my size. And that, of course, made it my fault.

You can see, I hope, how the real me was compromised. I began to work on my weight as if it were a divine calling. I took a personal, private oath: I decided to become somebody else, a thin somebody else. What's more, a thirty-three-billion-dollar weight-loss industry is proof that I'm not the only one who did so.

How about you? When did you discover some shameful, shocking secret about your physical body or appearance and decide you were of less value because of it? Have you ever looked in the mirror and in disgust believed that the quality of your life would be so much better if you just looked different? Have you placed more worth in your looks than in your character? Has the shape of your lips, the size of your hips, the tilt of your nose, or the texture of your hair ever dictated whether or not you applied for a job, hoped for attention from the opposite sex, or shared Christ with someone?

Look back through your own life. When did you declare war against yourself and determine that you'd be somebody other than your real, genetically authentic self? When did you decide God would love you more or better if only some physical feature of your body were changed or eliminated altogether?

What is it? Do you feel that your skin has too many blemishes? Do you have a short, "pugged" nose? Are your legs too long? Too short? Do you have a thick trunk? Freckles? We can each find something about ourselves that isn't quite perfect. But how much of the real you has to suffer?

I was forty-five when I finally made a pact of peace with my body. That pact was based on one simple fact—*God loves me.* He loves me not because of how I look, but because He understands my physical body far better than I do. He loves you, too. And since He was the one who designed genetic codes to be deeply embedded within each of us, why do we allow the cultural standards of what constitutes beauty to dictate our worth? God's love has never been limited to a perfect, a select—or slender—few. His love is measured by the price He was willing to pay to provide a way for us to live in relationship to Him. He sent His Son, Jesus, to die for our sins, not our appearance. He took our sins on Himself, not our size.

The real you needs you to come to peace with and to honor your physical body. It is, after all, the only earthly body in which your true self will ever live.

If you have turned yourself inside-out over your appearance, it's time to stop. No one knows better than me how difficult it is to make such a transition. Such a change isn't very popular in our modern culture. By contrast there are a multitude of programs, organizations, and even surgical procedures offering to help us conform to the world's standards of "beauty."

Honoring Your Body

How can you begin to honor your physical body instead of struggling against it? Consider these steps:

Accept your body.
Psalm 139:14-16 says:

> I praise you because I am fearfully and wonderfully made; your works are wonderful, I know that full well. My frame was not hidden from you when I was made in the secret place. When I was woven together in the depths of the earth, your eyes saw my unformed body.

Your body is miraculous. All you have to do is consider the digestive system, the nervous system, or how the muscles work, and you will quickly see what a magnificent machine the human body is. If you accidentally cut yourself, you can watch the healing take place within a few days. Get a tiny foreign substance in your eye, and immediately your body manufactures extra tears to flush it out and protect your eyesight. Just a tiny splinter in a finger sends defensive mechanisms into alert status. Most amazing of all, the body does all this without regard to whether you've been "good," or fit your own notion of perfection.

Your body is a gift from God. In total secret, within your mother's womb, He watched as your members were being knit into what other people now recognize as you. The Bible says He knows the end from the beginning, so even as a tiny baby, whether a sickly, healthy, or pudgy one, He saw your body just as it is today. He knew the color of your skin, the size of your feet, and the shape of your ears. He counts the hairs on your head and knows the length between the knuckles and joints on your fingers and toes.

He knows if your body craves chocolate or salty chips. He knows what size you are genetically predisposed to be. He knows if you are sensitive to the sun's rays or if you are unfazed by them. He knows your body inside and out. He designed it and He gave it to you as a gift. A miraculous gift. Accept it. Then thank Him for it.

Respect your body.
In 1 Corinthians 6:19-20, Paul says:

> Do you not know that your body is a temple of the Holy Spirit, who is in you, whom you have received from God? You are not your own; you were bought at a price. Therefore honor God with your body.

As with any valuable gift, you need to respect your body. Listen to its signals. Is it tired? Give it rest. Is it hungry? It's time to eat. Is it stressed? Then it's time for a vacation or for exercise.

For me, the ability to respect my body came when I looked

back over my dieting history and body image war. I couldn't believe how much I had done to my body in order to get it to change to suit me. For years I punished my body with deprivation, surgeries, and self-induced starvation. I wore tight corsets and girdles, and took unmentionable amounts of drugs and over-the-counter pills.

All that changed when I began to respect my body. I became more careful of what I did and didn't give my precious, miraculous machine. I began to choose my food more wisely, fueling my body more carefully.

Respecting our bodies doesn't mean giving in to their every whim. We don't cave in to sexual desires outside of marriage. We don't let ourselves become addicted to substances or chemicals. In this way, we honor God with our bodies. Keeping our physical selves clean and pure also means our authentic selves have clean houses in which to live.

Remember: Our bodies are intended to bless and honor God. We've only been assigned as caretakers of them. Once we belong to Christ, our bodies also belong to Him. As good stewards, we honor God when we respect our bodies.

Protect your body.
Your body is a gift to accept, respect, and protect. How you treat your physical self is a test of stewardship. In an admonition to a young man he considered his spiritual son, Paul writes these words:

Guard what has been entrusted to your care.

1 TIMOTHY 6:20

God has trusted you with a physical body, His most magnif-icently designed creation. He gave it to you to care for and pro-tect.

Is your body sick? Then in the spirit of stewardship, give it the best medical attention possible. Call for the elders of your church and get prayer for healing. Is your body out of shape? Then in the same spirit of stewardship, give it some exercise. Does your body demand more sleep? Then cut back on your schedule.

To protect our bodies, many of us have had to address such issues as secondhand smoke, dangerous working environ-ments, domestic violence, and sexual abuse. Do you care enough about your body to make the changes necessary in your own life and surroundings to protect your body from harm? Are there habits you need to address, such as smoking, overwork, or too much saturated fat in your daily diet?

Does the way you treat your body reflect an attitude of acceptance, respect, and protection for the beautiful gift God gave you in your physical body? Isn't it time you took a moment to thank God for His incredible gift? Let Him reas-sure you that your physical body is of His design and is most suitable for housing your true self. You no longer have to try to look like someone other than yourself. Your body is guaran-teed for a lifetime—your lifetime. It's the only one you'll get here on this earth. Your true self needs you to stop rejecting its house.

Someday, the Bible promises, we will be changed and live in immortal bodies. But for now let me challenge you with more words from the apostle Paul to Timothy. These words were written to charge Timothy in areas of ministry, but I offer these same words to you as good advice in accepting, respecting, and protecting your physical body as well:

> Guard the good deposit that was entrusted to you—guard it with the help of the Holy Spirit who lives in us.
>
> 2 TIMOTHY 1:14

Deny your true self no longer. Be who you are. Look like you look. Stop judging yourself by some unreachable, irresponsible standard of perfection or beauty. Give yourself permission to have a healthy, responsible attitude toward your body. Your body is not your enemy; it is a very personal and individual gift. Accept it as your gift from God. Honor God by respecting it, serve Him by protecting it. Let the Holy Spirit guide you. The real you will appreciate it very much.

Never forget: Just as your true self is a work of God, your body is His creative masterpiece. Become an admirer of His handiwork, instead of a critic. Your body will thank you for it, and your true self will love it, too.

Personal Reflection

1. If you were to reflect on one thing that you hate about your body, what would it be? If you were to ask God to help you love that feature, would He have to change that feature or your heart attitude? Which would be more likely?

2. Choose one major area of your physical well-being that needs attention. What responsibility could you take to bet-

ter care for yourself in that area? Write one simple commitment you can make to self-care in that area.

3. If you were to truly respect your body, what habit(s) would you need to break? What could help you with that? Who?

4. How can you better protect the body you have chosen to accept and respect? Do you need more rest? More relaxation? More recreation?

5. Is there someone else who shows a lack of acceptance or respect, or who doesn't protect your body? How can you bring an end to such destruction and the disrespect of someone else? Do you need help? Who can you ask for that help?

6. Write a prayer of thanksgiving to God concerning your physical body. Appreciate how it works, and tell God of your concern about anything that is wrong with it and then, in love, begin to bless your body—that's right—in writing!

Prayerful Response

Lord, I choose today to honor my body. I know it's the only body I'll get here on earth and it was designed to last me a lifetime. Give me the strength to choose whole, healthy ways to honor my body. Show me how to stop whatever destructive practices I've taken on and give me wisdom to manage my body responsibly. I make a commitment before You to accept, respect, and protect my body. Amen.

Honoring God From the Heart of the Real Me

Sheri is in her early forties. She didn't set out to make it happen, but her whole life has been spent looking for her real self. Unfortunately, she looked in all the wrong places, and a string of unsuccessful relationships with men has left her tired, broken, and bitter.

"Now," she admits, "I see my daughter headed down the same pathway I took. I now have custody of my eleven-month-old granddaughter, and what's more, my mother is very ill and I have to care for her, too. Not only have I lost pieces of my true self at every step along the way, but to tell you the truth, finding the time or the energy to take care of myself right now is out of the question."

Sheri's case is not that unusual. Many women find themselves carrying far too much responsibility, for far too long, with little relief—much less the chance to pursue their true desires and dreams. Life itself becomes exhausting, and for some even hopeless.

And yet … if we do not take care of our own authentic selves, we will be crushed under life's load. Only as we find help in meeting our own needs will we be able to meet the needs of those who depend on us. Yet we must first care *about* ourselves in order to care *for* ourselves.

When Sheri told me of her situation, I immediately urged her to reach out for help. In her case, she was able to find a program that offered to send volunteers who could give her a break from caring for her mother. A neighbor happily agreed to watch the baby at the same time, allowing her space to rest, to walk, or to go out alone.

Perhaps your situation is not as crushing as Sheri's, but it does become overwhelming from time to time. Maybe you don't feel like you are on the wrong highway altogether, but that life seems to keep tossing frustrating roadblocks in your way.

Lynette's husband pastors a small but growing home-missions church. "Last week we had to let our associate pastor go. His wife worked in the church office, so we didn't just lose one staff member, we lost two. There's no way around it—all of her work has fallen back on me for a while."

Lynette had been pursuing some of her God-given dreams before this unavoidable responsibility landed in her lap. "Right now," she admits, "taking care of my own needs is the farthest thing from my mind."

And yet, Lynette has found a place to go to find constant

inner refreshment. A place where there is sweet water for her soul … and for every soul that faces the wearying demands of life.

"Right now, I am finding so much renewal … so much life in the time I spend alone with God. I need this time with Him. I crave the early morning times when I can be fed by the Bible … and also my late-night cup of tea, when I can sit alone with God and, for just a few minutes, let God love me."

Lynette knows there will be times again when life is freer— when she again will be able to pursue the things God has uniquely given her to do. Yet she also knows this: The most important thing she can do for herself is to renew her soul. "If I didn't do that," says Lynette, "I wouldn't survive."

Something to Give …

My objective throughout this book has been to help you to live life as your true self. Too many of us have looked at, and defined, ourselves by our roles, rules, and responsibilities. I hope you are discovering that life is better approached when we view and define these things from the perspective of our true selves.

Many women are discovering the strength, peace, and new meaning that comes from this transformed perspective.

Abby is a good example. Her husband recently started a new business, and that has brought new pressure into her life. "Everything happens at home," she explained. "Board meetings, planning sessions, employees coming and going…. For the next few months I see no likelihood of letup or a return to regular hours. The phone starts ringing before we are finished with breakfast."

Still, Abby makes it top priority to seek renewal of her inner self.

"When I'm overloaded," she says, "I just say, 'Hold everything.' I go for long walks—as much as a mile or two. Sometimes I take along my Bible, or a book, and sit on a park bench for a while. Sometimes I just pray and think … just stare off into the blue of the sky, or watch the birds and squirrels. It's like getting my batteries recharged.

"When I get back home, I have something to give again."

The apostle Paul has told us,

Therefore, I urge you, brothers, in view of God's mercy, to offer your bodies as living sacrifices, holy and pleasing to God—this is your spiritual act of worship. Do not conform any longer to the pattern of this world, but be transformed by the renewing of your mind. Then you will be able to test and approve what God's will is—his good, pleasing and perfect will.

ROMANS 12:1-2

Some of us have merely lost ourselves amid life's demands. Others of us have sacrificed ourselves until there is nothing left to give. That is not what God intends. God gives, renews, fills, and replenishes, so that we can continually experience nurturing life within us. This is God's way, a way of living that you cannot know unless you know and live in constant contact with

God, who loves us. The world doesn't just say "me first," it says "me only." God wants us to take care of our own needs so that we can reach out to others from our true, healthy self.

Paul gives us more on this matter:

> For by the grace given me I say to every one of you: Do not think of yourself more highly than you ought, but rather think of yourself with sober judgment, in accordance with the measure of faith God has given you.
>
> ROMANS 12:3

We use sober judgment while rediscovering our authentic selves. We honor our true needs. Then we wholly present ourselves to God. That's what we need to be about. Seeking God's plan and design for your true self isn't pride or arrogance—it is living as a whole person.

Consider the first commandment, which says:

> Love the Lord your God with all your heart and with all your soul and with all your strength.
>
> DEUTERONOMY 6:5

Serving God wholly means loving Him—not with just a single piece, not with parts, but with the entire, whole, and integrated self. Can we love God with all our heart, soul, and strength if there are missing parts of each? The way to serve Him truly, happily, is to grow in personal authenticity.

The Difference

If you have decided to be authentic, it's important to know what you are about. To some degree it's also important to learn what others mean by *authentic,* so that you don't get stuck in self-centered and limiting definitions of your own.

Recently, I asked Christian women how they would describe the false person, and how they would describe the authentic person. When it came to defining false, or nonauthentic people, their responses included those who:

- are people-pleasers rather than God-pleasers;
- are discontent with who they are or their talents and gifts;
- are ill at ease with, or even denying, their limitations and abilities;
- are caught up in appearances and "proper" or acceptable behaviors;
- are self-seeking, attention grabbing, emotionally needy, and self-centered;
- define themselves by their dirty house, checkbook balance, gray hair, bad complexion, or body size;
- compromise to "fit in," rather than be their honest selves; and
- settle for and depend on the opinions of others for their sense of self and worth.

On the other hand, when it came to characterizing those who are learning to live according to their authentic self, they included:

- being true to your inner self and disciplining your behavior to match;
- having enough personal confidence to stand by convictions;
- being the same person when alone as when in the company of others;
- not being afraid of the truth about yourself;
- being able to say you're sorry when you've been wrong;
- being confident enough in yourself not to unduly compare yourself to others—and keeping Christ as your standard;
- being confident enough to inspire greatness in others without being jealous or needing to claim the credit;
- being confident enough to warn others when you see them doing wrong;
- being secure enough to be different—even to appear eccentric in order to remain true to who you are;
- being genuine, with no airs or pretense;
- having the ability to reveal unpleasant or weak areas, and admit faults when appropriate;
- understanding that "except for the grace of God, there go I"—that without Christ you can do nothing, but in Him you are able to do everything He directs;
- having a thankful, grateful attitude—even during tough times;
- not being afraid to give your honest opinion or express genuine feelings;
- being a responsible steward in areas of money, time, and even love; and
- being a person who responds to life out of who you are, rather than what you do.

These women also told me that the most personally authentic women they knew lived with deep peace, contentment, and rest. They also have a healthy ability to trust, and they are truthful and definite about their feelings and needs.

It comes down to this: The woman who learns to seek God—God first, God only—will hear within her the one voice that will lead her out of the trap of being a "pleaser," under the rule of others and their needs, and into the freedom of being whole, strong, and at peace. She will at last become an authentic woman before God.

Emerging

For those of us who have decided to reclaim our real selves, we know that falseness and pretense, or the harried life, is not what God intends. No, God has another plan. He wants us to emerge as new women. Listen to these often quoted words from Jeremiah, with the true self you are becoming in mind:

> "For I know the plans I have for you," declares the Lord, "plans to prosper you and not to harm you, plans to give you hope and a future. Then you will call upon me and come and pray to me, and I will listen to you. You will seek me and find me when you seek me with all your heart."
>
> JEREMIAH 29:11-13

As we learn to connect with God from our authentic self, something changes deep inside. As our soul comes to life, so will our connection to God. We will come to love prayer.

Instead of merely hoping God hears us, we will know that God listens to our prayers because we will no longer be offering halfhearted words, but seeking Him with our whole, true selves. Something new and wonderful will happen in our everyday life. His hope, and His future plan for us will begin to unroll at our feet. We will not only connect with God and ourselves, but also connect in a new way with people. Jesus showed us this when a so-called expert in Jewish law tested Him with a question:

> "Teacher, which is the greatest commandment in the Law?" Jesus replied: "'Love the Lord your God with all your heart and with all your soul and with all your mind.' This is the first and greatest commandment. And the second is like it: 'Love your neighbor as yourself.'"
>
> MATTHEW 22:36-39

First, we go to God for the inner replenishment only He can give. When we do this we become free from our own inner needs because God has filled them, and we no longer must struggle to cradle, coddle, or quiet the weak, needy person inside. As whole people, we can give to others without denying or draining ourselves.

The apostle Paul seems to have lived as a whole, authentic self, as a man who sought inner life from God first, and then allowed God's life to live in him. He wrote:

> First, I thank my God through Jesus Christ for all of you, because your faith is being reported all over the world. God,

whom I serve with my whole heart in preaching the gospel
of his Son, is my witness how constantly I remember you in
my prayers at all times.

ROMANS 1:8-9

Paul took up the responsibility for seeking God with his
whole heart first. Then, directed by God, he faced the world
and its needs. Women who are emerging in God-given authenticity will do what Paul did: they will take up the responsibility
to seek God with their whole hearts first. Then, directed by
God, they will face the world, with its needs.

New Woman in the Mirror

What we have just seen is a grand pattern God uses to help us
grow as His own true daughters. Many of us have lived in
opposition to this pattern. We've become focused on people
and their needs, and only when we've been drained have we
sought God. Now we know we must build a new habit, seeking God before all else.

What changes can we expect as this new pattern transforms
our lives? Here is a glimpse of the new you that will begin to
emerge:

**You will become more confident that you are living close
to God and serving Him as He directs your steps.**
In the Old Testament we read:

What does the Lord your God ask of you but to fear the
Lord your God, to walk in all his ways, to love him, to serve
[him] with all your heart and with all your soul, and to
observe [his] commands and decrees ... for your own good?

DEUTERONOMY 10:12-13

**You will live in obedience to God and His Word, and trust
in His provision.**

If you faithfully obey the commands I am giving you
today—to love ... God and to serve him with all your heart
and with all your soul—then I will send rain on your land in
its season ... so that you ... will eat and be satisfied.

DEUTERONOMY 11:13-15

**You will learn to rely on the wisdom of God in all life's
challenges.**
As the writer of Proverbs insists:

Trust in the Lord with all your heart and lean not on your
own understanding; in all your ways acknowledge him, and
he will make your paths straight.

PROVERBS 3:5-6

**Because you trust God first, above all else, you will stop
insisting on the support, permission, or affirmation of
others as you live your life to the glory of God alone.**
Paul insisted:

Whatever you do, work at it with all your heart, as working for the Lord, not for men.

COLOSSIANS 3:23

This is the heritage of the daughters of God. It is your heritage.

Tested ... Like Gold

As we near the end of this book, I want to encourage you with the whole truth. As you become more authentic, life will not automatically become easier. The true self will be tested.

Choosing personal authenticity doesn't guarantee freedom from pain, challenge, wounding, or confusion. But it is the pathway to wisdom and inner peace, as the work that requires your whole lifetime begins. Though this may seem daunting to many, with Paul I have the confidence to assure you:

He who began a good work in you [and in me] will carry it on to completion until the day of Christ Jesus.

PHILIPPIANS 1:6

Bringing His work to completion will require you to pass through testing. Testing is nothing new for those who follow God closely. He tests His own, because that is the way He matures us. But along with James I say:

Consider it pure joy, my [sisters], whenever you face trials of many kinds, because you know that the testing of your faith develops perseverance. Perseverance must finish its work so that you may be mature and complete, not lacking anything.

JAMES 1:2-4

The goal, as we now know, is to live with our service to others coming out of a true picture of ourselves. So we let our doing come out of our being ... knowing that our being is made complete by our doing. Just like the man James wrote about:

You see that his faith and his actions were working together, and his faith was made complete by what he did.

JAMES 2:22

Fortunately, God does not expect us to walk through this life of testing and growth on our own.

Relying on the Help of Others

God, in His goodness, places people in our lives to help us grow and get ready. It's up to us to avail ourselves of their counsel and support. Paul wrote:

Praise be to the God and Father of our Lord Jesus Christ, the Father of compassion and the God of all comfort, who comforts us in all our troubles, so that we can comfort those in any trouble with the comfort we ourselves have received from God. For just as the sufferings of Christ flow over into our lives, so also through Christ our comfort overflows.

2 CORINTHIANS 1:3-5

In this passage, we learn about the wonderful way God comforts us in our life of growth—that is, through the compassion of others who have struggled to grow and emerge in wholeness, just as we struggle. God knows how to place wise counselors in our lives, not for our purposes, but to direct us in ways that will fulfill His purposes.

No doubt, there are women around you right now who have already encountered similar situations to the very ones you are facing. Reach out to those women. Ask for advice. Ask them how they handled pressured situations like yours. Ask them if they can see His greater purposes in your life, which you may not be able to see right now.

Eventually, you will turn and find that other women are following after you, walking on paths like those you've walked, and they will need to draw wisdom from your experiences. And if you walk the path to authentic selfhood, you will be given the wisdom to pass on, because you will be tried like gold.

Going on From Here

Early in this book, I told you about things I gave up because others pressured me. Thankfully, God has helped to restore the real me over the years. It's been a long process and it's still ongoing. But I want to close by telling you what He's done in my life, so you can be assured He will do the same for you.

Once, I gave up daydreaming, but God has wonderfully restored my imagination, allowing me to write fiction, dream of new ways to minister to people in prayer, and decorate.

I gave up my acceptance of my body, incorporating unhealthy ways to try to get rid of hated fat and unwanted weight. But when I let God help me rediscover the real me, He also restored a sense of self-worth that is based on knowing His love for me, something that will not end when this body gives out and I must step into eternity to be with Him.

And God has taught me much more.

When I find myself serving out of a false or expected self, my "well" soon dries up. Within a short period of time, I begin to resent the very ones I'm commanded to love and serve. I have found, even though it sounds contrary to the way I was raised and trained for ministry, that to effectively minister to others, I have to take the responsibility for caring for myself first. To do otherwise is to be like the doctor who is sick with the flu and who sneezes full in the face of his patient.

The more I tend to the needs of the real me, the less important it becomes for others to take care of me. This makes reaching out to others much easier. The opposite is also true. The less attention I pay to my real inner me, letting pressures and problems build, the less able I am to reach out to others and the more I want and expect others to take care of me.

I have also discovered that the more comfortable I become in my own company (solitude), the more comfortable I am in the company of others. Again, the opposite is also true: the less time I spend in my own company, becoming more comfortable with who and what I am, the less comfortable I am in the company of others. Only as I dared to discover who I was and what a good friend I could be did I realize that others did honestly like me and want me around.

Finally, I know for sure that God has no favorites. God can wonderfully restore what has been lost to you. Your wonderful gifts, talents, and ministry can be rediscovered and flow as freely as if there had been no interruption. No matter what you've been through, I know this: God loves you and has a wonderful real you waiting for you to discover. The real you He created you to be can start to blossom today.

And now we come to the end—but for you this can be a new beginning. The adventure of becoming personally authentic and living your life to the full lies ahead of you, holding the promise of a lifetime of growth and excitement.

In a very important way, you are the conclusion to this book. For I never intended this to be a book that was over when you turned the last page. This book—or at least its purposes—will be completed only as you grow closer to God and allow Him to help you emerge as your true self. With that in mind, I encourage you to turn to your journal one more time, and let these questions begin to direct your steps as you become the authentic woman God made you to be.

Personal Reflection

1. As if you were preparing to stand in front of a group, write an explanation of who you are, what you believe, and how God desires to use you in the lives of others. Are you writing more statements about doing or being?
2. What is needed to bring your life into more being/doing balance? Where could you get that? Who could help you?

3. Who do you know that is closer to being an authentic person than you feel yourself to be at the moment? What would you have to do to build a better relationship with that person?

4. Who might benefit from your friendship and example as she works to reclaim the "real me"? What would you have to do to build a better relationship with that person?

5. How has this book helped you to know what happened to your real me?

If you'd like to write and tell me about this, I'd love to know about it.

My address is:

Neva Coyle
P.O. Box 1638
Oakhurst, CA 93644

Prayerful Response

Thank You, dear Father, for holding my real me in reserve until I was ready to reclaim her. Thank You for not giving up on me when I and many others did. Thank You for revealing the real me You created me to be and helping me grow and become that person. Lord, I covenant with You to live, with Your help, as the real me, for Your glory. Amen.

NOTES

FOUR
In the Company of One

1. Anthony Storr, *Solitude* (New York: Ballantine, a division of Random House, Inc., 1988), xiv.

SEVEN
Changing the Real Me

1. Marsha Sinetar, *Elegant Choices, Healing Choices* (New York: Paulist Press, 1988), 34.
2. Marsha Sinetar, *Ordinary People as Monks and Mystics* (New York: Paulist Press, 1986), 27.
3. Sinetar, *Ordinary People,* 4.

EIGHT
Honoring the Real Me

1. Sinetar, *Ordinary People,* 13.

NINE
Nurturing the Real Me

1. If you need more help in establishing biblically based boundaries in your life, I recommend you read *Boundaries,* by Dr. Henry Cloud and Dr. John Townsend (Grand Rapids, Mich.: Zondervan, 1992).

Also by Neva Coyle

Free to be Slim

Success is defined as a lifestyle – not a size. Discover
how you can be a new person – spiritually, emotionally
and physically – by following this lifestyle approach to
diet, nutrition, health and body image.

Thousands of men and women have already found
their way to freedom from overeating and food abuse
through this million-copy bestselling book.

Loved on a Grander Scale

Do you know what it is like to lose the same twenty
pounds, over and over again? Does your weight make
you feel unlovable, ugly or ashamed? If it does, then
Neva Coyle can identify with you.

In Neva's own words:
'This book isn't about returning to undisciplined eating.
Not in the least! It goes beyond eating. It goes beyond
weight. In fact it goes all the way to the cross. It's about
finding worth and purpose far beyond physical size or
appearance.'

 **Kingsway Publications**